ROUND-UP

CONTENTS

Introduction

Round-up Grammar Practice 2 combines games and fun with serious, systematic grammar practice. It is ideal for students at the early stages of English language learning.

Students see grammar points clearly presented in colourful boxes and tables. They practise grammar through lively, highly illustrated games and activities.

Round-up is especially designed for different students studying English in different ways.

It can be used:
● in class with a coursebook. Students do both oral work – in pairs and in groups – and written work in Round-up.
● after class. The 'write-in' activities are ideal for homework. Students can practise what they have learned in the classroom.
● in the holidays for revision. Round-up has clear instructions and simple grammar boxes, so students can study at home without a teacher.

The Round-up Teacher's Guide includes a full answer key and four progress tests plus answer keys.

Addison Wesley Longman Limited
Edinburgh Gate, Harlow
Essex CM20 2JE, England
and Associated Companies throughout the world.

First published in 1992 by A. Vlachos - "Express Publishing".
This edition first published by Longman Group Limited 1995.
Eighth impression 1997.

Printed in Spain
by Mateu Cromo

Ilustrated by Chris Zmertis

ISBN 0582 25620 8

7 **First say and then write questions and answers as in the example:**

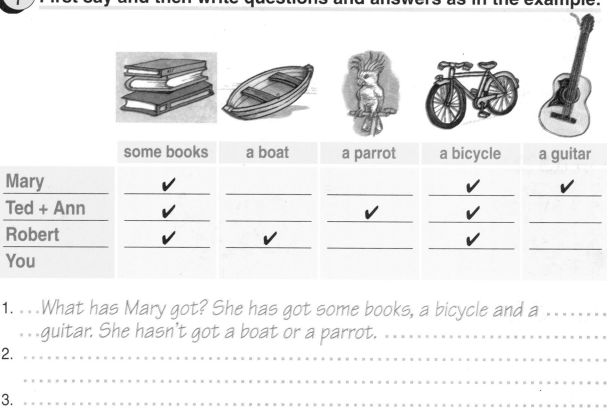

	some books	a boat	a parrot	a bicycle	a guitar
Mary	✔			✔	✔
Ted + Ann	✔		✔	✔	
Robert	✔	✔		✔	
You					

1. ....What has Mary got? She has got some books, a bicycle and a ....
....guitar. She hasn't got a boat or a parrot. ....

2. ....
....

3. ....

4. What have you got? I ....
....

Short answers

Have **you** got a car?	Yes, I / we have.	No, I / we haven't.
Has **he / she / it** got a car?	Yes, he / she / it has.	No, he / she / it hasn't.
Have **they** got a car?	Yes, they have.	No, they haven't.

8 **Ask and answer as in the example :**

1. they / a TV?
.Have they got a TV?
.No, they haven't....
.They've got a radio.

2. he / a bag?
....
....
....

1. The Verb "can"

3. they / dogs?

....
....
....

4. it / wings?

....
....
....

5. the girl / a tomato?

....
....
....

6. the boys / a ball?

....
....
....

7. the boy / an umbrella?

....
....
....

8. the dog / a bone?

....
....
....

The Verb "can"

Affirmative	Negative		Interrogative
	Long form	Short form	
I can	I cannot	I can't	Can I?
You can	You cannot	You can't	Can you?
He can	He cannot	He can't	Can he?
She can	She cannot	She can't	Can she?
It can	It cannot	It can't	Can it?
We can	We cannot	We can't	Can we?
You can	You cannot	You can't	Can you?
They can	They cannot	They can't	Can they?

Short Answers		
	Can you drive?	Yes, I can.
		No, I can't.

9 Ask and answer as in the example :

MMMM!

1. (walk) ..*Can he walk?*.
   ...*No, he can't.*.....

2. (talk) ....

3. (cook) ....

4. (watch TV) .... 5. (swim) .... 6. (read) ....

....

7. (fly) .... 8. (sleep) .... 9. (sing) ....

....

10 **Ask and answer as in the example :**

	sing	draw	dance	play the guitar
Jane	✔		✔	
Chris		✔		✔
Liz + Brian	✔		✔	
You				

1. ..*Can Jane sing? Yes, she can. Can she draw? No, she can't. Can she* ....
   ..*dance? Yes, she can. Can she play the guitar? No, she can't. So,* ....
   ..*Jane can sing and dance but she can't draw or play the guitar.* ....

2. ....

....

....

3. ....

....

....

4. ....

....

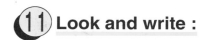 **Look and write :**

Name:	Mary Taylor	*She is Mary Taylor.* ......
Nationality:	American	*She is American.* ....
Job:	singer	*She is a singer.* ....
Hair:	blonde	*She has got blonde hair*
Eyes:	blue	*and blue eyes.* ....
Abilities:	sing, dance	*She can sing and dance.*

Name:	Simon Flower	. . . .
Nationality:	British	. . . .
Job:	teacher	. . . .
Hair:	black	. . . .
Eyes:	green	. . . .
Abilities:	swim, drive	. . . .

YOU

Name:	. . . .	. . . .
Nationality:	. . . .	. . . .
Job:	. . . .	. . . .
Hair:	. . . .	. . . .
Eyes:	. . . .	. . . .
Abilities:	. . . .	. . . .

1. The Verb "can"

Guessing Game 1

Your teacher divides the class into two groups. Then he /she asks a student to come to the front of the class. The teacher whispers a verb e.g "write" into his / her ear. The students, by asking questions, try to guess what he/she can do. The group which finds out wins.

Group A S1:	Can you dive?	Group A S2:	Can you swim?
Leader:	No, I can't.	Leader:	No, I can't.
Group B S1:	Can you play tennis?	Group B S2:	Can you write?
Leader:	No, I can't.	Leader:	Yes, I can.

Group B gets 1 point. Choose another leader and play the game again.

2. Personal Pronouns

Competition Game 2

Your teacher divides the class into two groups. Play the game as follows:

Teacher :	Pam		Group B S1 :	he
Group A S1 :	she		Teacher :	Mary and I
Teacher :	Chris		Group A S2 :	they
			Teacher :	Wrong! We. Group A doesn't get a point.

Each correct answer gets 1 point. The group with the most points is the winner.

3. The Verb "to be"

Guessing Game 3

Your teacher divides the class into two groups, chooses a leader and asks him/her to think of a job. Then the groups in turn try to guess what his/her job is.

Group A S1 :	Are you a teacher?		Leader :	No, I'm not.
Leader :	No, I'm not.		Group A S2 :	Are you a butcher?
Group B S1 :	Are you a singer?		Leader :	Yes, I am. etc.

Group A is the winner. Choose another leader and play the game again.

4. The Verb "to have"

Guessing Game 4a

Your teacher divides the class into two groups, chooses a leader and asks him/her to think of 5 items he/she has got and write them on a piece of paper. Then the groups in turn try to find what the leader has got by asking only ten questions. The group which has found most or all of the things the leader has got is the winner.

Group A S1 :	Have you got an umbrella?		Group A S2 :	Have you got a bag?
Leader :	Yes, I have.		Leader :	No, I haven't.
Group B S1 :	Have you got a cat?		Group B S2 :	Have you got a dog?
Leader :	No, I haven't.		Leader :	Yes, I have. etc.

Never-ending Game 4b

One student starts saying what he/she has got. The next student goes on to say what the previous student has got adding what he/she has got.

S1 : I've got a dog.
S2 : He's got a dog and I've got a cat.
S3 : She's got a cat and I've got a bag.   etc.

Plurals / This - These / That - Those

A Most nouns form their plural by adding "s".

cameras, chairs, snakes, parrots, doctors.

12 Fill in the plural as in the example :

1. one apple-two *apples*   2. one bird-two ....   3. one shoe-two ....

4. one dolphin-two ....   5. one clown-two ....   6. one spider-two ....

B Nouns ending in s, ss, sh, ch, x and o take "es" in the plural.

bus - buses	brush - brushes	box - boxes
glass - glasses	match - matches	potato - potatoes

BUT:

radio - radios, piano - pianos, photo - photos, video - videos

13 Fill in the plural as in the example:

1. one watch-two *watches*   2. one fox-two ....   3. one mosquito-two ......

4. one bench-two . . . .   5. one dress-two . . . .   6. one witch-two . . . .

 Nouns ending in a consonant + y ⟹ ies

Nouns ending in a vowel (a,e,i,o,u) + y ⟹ ys

city - cities	**BUT**	boy - boys

14 **Fill in the plural as in the example:**

1. one toy-three .. *toys* ...   2. one lady- two . . . .   3. one baby-two . . . .

4. one family-two . . . .   5. one diary-two . . . .   6. one fly-two . . . .

 Some nouns ending in f / fe ⟹ ves

thief - thieves	knife - knives	**BUT**	roof - roofs

15 **Fill in the plural as in the example:**

1. one leaf-two .. *leaves*   2. one loaf-two . . . .   3. one wolf-two . . . .

13

Irregular Plurals

tooth - teeth	mouse - mice	ox - oxen	child - children
fish - fish	deer - deer	sheep - sheep	woman - women
foot - feet	goose - geese	man - men	

16 **Fill in the plural as in the example:**

1. one child-two ... *children*   2. one mouse-two ....   3. one fish-two ....

4. one tooth-two ....   5. one goose-three ....   6. one policeman-two ......

Note: Adjectives take no "s" in the plural.   e.g. an old book - old books

17 **Write the words in the plural and in the correct column.**

party - banana - tomato - room - day - wife - sandwich
story - bus - class - radio - fly - knife - lady - leaf

-s	-es	-ies	-ves
..radios....			

18 **Complete as in the example:**

1. A pen. Two ..... *pens*.............   2. A bus. Ten ....
3. A cowboy. Two ....   4. A woman. Two ....
5. A house. Three ....   6. A fish. Three ....

7. A tooth. Five . . . . 8. A key. Four . . . .

9. A spy. Two . . . . 10. A picture. Three . . . .

11. A letter. Three . . . . 12. A shirt. Two . . . .

13. A table. Two . . . . 14. A child. Two . . . .

15. A girl. Four . . . . 16. A class. Three . . . .

17. A tail. Two . . . . 18. A disc jockey. Two . . . .

19. A sheep. Ten . . . . 20. A zebra. Two . . . .

(19) Change to the plural as in the example:

The dog is in the garden. . . . . . . *The dogs are in the garden.* . . . .

1. He is a tall man. . . . .

2. It is a potato. . . . .

3. It is a beautiful dress. . . . .

4. The glass is on the table. . . . .

5. It is a tooth. . . . .

6. The baby is in the bedroom. . . . .

7. You are a nice child. . . . .

8. She is a housewife. . . . .

9. It is a leaf. . . . .

10. It is a monkey. . . . .

F   Some nouns are uncountable. They have no plural. These are:

bread	cheese	jam	milk
lemonade	tea	wine	Coca-Cola
butter	coffee	meat	sugar
money	water	wood	paper

Note: **A / an** is not used with uncountable nouns. **Some** is used instead.

We say: **a cup**   **BUT**   **some bread**

(20) Fill in the blanks with "a", "an" or "some".

1. . . *some* . . water   2. . . . . dolphin   3. . . . . sugar   4. . . . . flag

5. .... cheese

6. .... meat

7. .... orange

8. .... money

9. .... shirt

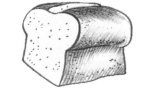

10. .... bread

11. .... coffee

12. .... doll

13. .... butter

14. .... milk

15. .... sailor

16. .... jam

G Uncountable nouns can be made countable by using these words:

a bottle
of milk

a glass
of water

a cup
of tea

a loaf
of bread

a slice
of bread

a packet
of tea

a jar
of jam

a can
of Coke

a piece
of cheese

a bowl
of sugar

a carton
of milk

a kilo
of meat

21 **Fill in the correct word as in the example:**

1. Three *glasses* of water.   2. Two .... of sugar.   3. Two .... of bread.

4. Three ...... of bread.   5. Two ...... of beer.   6. Two .... of wine.

7. Two ...... of cake.   8. Three ...... of tea.   9. Three ...... of Coke.

10. Two ...... of coffee.   11. Three ...... of jam.   12. Three ...... of cheese.

22 **Fill in the plural as in the example:**

1. A dog. Three .... *dogs.* ....   12. A lady. Three ....
2. Some sugar. Two .... of sugar.   13. A child. Three ....
3. A church. Two ....   14. Some beer. Two .... of beer.
4. A team. Two ....   15. Some water. Two .... of water.
5. Some bread. Three .... of bread.   16. A day. Five ....
6. Some cheese. Four .... of cheese.   17. Some tea. Three .... of tea.
7. A horse. Two ....   18. Some milk. Three .... of milk.
8. Some wine. Two .... of wine.   19. A goose. Two ....
9. A bicycle. Three ....   20. Some jam. Four .... of jam.
10. Some Coke. Two .... of Coke.   21. A mouse. Two ....
11. A boy. Three ....   22. Some meat. Two .... of meat.

This – These	That – Those
This (near) — **This** is a duck.	**That** (far) — **That** is a monkey.
These (near) — **These** are ducks.	**Those** (far) — **Those** are monkeys.

23 **Fill in the blanks with "This", "These", "That" or "Those".**

1. ..*This*..... is a candle.

2. .... are socks.

3. .... is a donkey.

4. .... are fish.

5. .... are hamburgers.

6. .... is a crocodile.

7. .... are spoons.

Guessing Game 5

The teacher chooses a leader and then divides the class into two groups, group A and group B. Then the teacher writes a singular or plural noun on a piece of paper (e.g. pencils) which he / she gives to the leader. Finally, the teacher invites the students to guess what he / she has written by asking the leader questions in turn. The students can ask the leader ten questions in order to find it. If the groups cannot guess within 10 questions, the game is a draw.

Group A S1:	Is it singular or plural?	Group A S2:	Are they pens?
Leader:	Plural.	Leader:	No, they aren't.
Group B S1:	Are they chairs?	Group B S2:	Are they pencils?
Leader:	No, they aren't.	Leader:	Yes, they are.

Competition Game 6

The teacher divides the class into two groups and says nouns in the singular. The groups in turn say the plural of each word. Each correct answer gets 1 point. The group with the most points is the winner.

Teacher :	cat	Teacher :	ox
Group A S1 :	cats	Group A S2 :	oxes
Teacher :	foot	Teacher :	Wrong! oxen. Group A doesn't
Group B S1 :	feet		get a point.

3. Possessives

Personal pronouns		Possessive adjectives	Possessive pronouns
(Before verbs as subjects)	(After verbs as objects)	(followed by nouns)	(not followed by nouns)
I	Me	My	Mine
You	You	Your	Yours
He / She / it	Him / Her / It	His / Her / Its	His / Hers / —
We	Us	Our	Ours
You	You	Your	Yours
They	Them	Their	Theirs

Possessive case with people

We use 's with one person.

the man's hat

We use s' with two or more persons.
the girls' skirts
BUT
the children's books,
the women's bags,
the men's umbrellas

Note: We also use 's with animals.
    the cat's tail

Possessive case with things

We use of with things.

the trunk of
the tree

(24) Look at the pictures and write as in the example:

Mary   umbrella

1. This is *Mary's* . . . . .
. . . *umbrella.* . . . .
It's *.her umbrella.* . . . . .
This *umbrella is hers.*. .

the girls   hats

2. These are . . . .
. . . .
They're . . . .
These . . . .

Ben   flowers

3. These are . . . .
. . . .
They're . . . .
These . . . .

the dog   bone

4. This is . . . .
. . . .
It's . . . .
. . . .

the tree   leaves

5. These are . . . .
. . . .
They're . . . .
. . . .

the tiger   teeth

6. These are . . . .
. . . .
They're . . . .
. . . .

Father   newspaper

7. This is . . . .
. . . .
It's . . . .
This . . . .

25 **Look at the pictures and write as in the example:**

1. I've got a basket.
   ..It's my basket...
   . . . .
   . . . .

2. He . . . .
   . . . .
   It's . . . .
   . . . .

3. You . . . .

   It's . . . .
   . . . .

4. Peter and I . . . .
   . . . .
   They're . . . .
   . . . .

5. They . . . .

   They're . . . .
   . . . .

6. The old lady . . . .

   It's . . . .
   . . . .

7. We . . . .
   . . . .
   It's . . . .

8. The man . . . .
   . . . .
   They're . . . .
   . . . .

26 **Underline the correct word as in the example:**

1. David is (my, mine) brother.
2. This house is (their, theirs).
3. It is Bob's cat. It's (his, her) cat.
4. These flowers are (your, yours).
5. This is (our, ours) garden. It's (our, ours).
6. This is Sally's car. It's (her, hers) car.
7. The blue skirt is (my, mine).
8. Mr Jones is (their, theirs) father.
9. (My, Mine) hat is green.
10. This is Bill's pen. It's (his, her) pen.

Game 7

Your teacher divides the class into two groups. Then he/she gives cues and each group in turn tries to say the correct possessive. Each correct answer gets 1 point. The group with the most points is the winner.

Teacher :	Mary / bag		Teacher :	woman / car
Group A S1 :	her bag		Group A S2 :	her car
Teacher :	children / books		Teacher :	I / pen
Group B S1 :	their books		Group B S2 :	my pen etc.

4. There is – are   a / some / any

	Affirmative		Negative		Interrogative
	Long form	**Short form**	**Long form**	**Short form**	
singular	There is	There's	There is not	There isn't	Is there?
plural	There are		There are not	There aren't	Are there?

27 Write "There is" or "There are" as in the example:

1) *There are* two swings in the garden.
2) .... a slide.
3) .... two children.
4) .... a woman.
5) .... a table.
6) .... two chairs.
7) .... lots of flowers.
8) .... a cat.
9) .... four birds.
10) .... a ball.
11) .... two trees.
12) .... a dog.

some + **countable** or **uncountable** noun (in **affirmative** sentences)	**any** + **countable** or **uncountable** noun (in **questions** and **negative** sentences)
There are **some** tomatoes. There is **some** bread.	Are there **any** oranges? Is there **any** milk? No, there isn't **any** milk.

28 Fill in "some" or "any".

1. Are there . *any* . children in the park?
2. Are there .... eggs on the table?
3. There are .... flowers in the garden.
4. There isn't .... meat in the shop.
5. There isn't .... bread in the cupboard.
6. There are .... apples on the tree.
7. There is .... wine in the bottle.
8. There is .... milk in the bottle.

4. There is - are   a / some / any

9. There isn't . . . . water in the glass.
11. There is . . . . tea in the teapot.
13. Are there . . . . children in the room?
15. There aren't . . . . . cars in the street.

10. There are . . . . potatoes on the table.
12. Is there . . . . chocolate in the fridge?
14. There is . . . . cheese on the plate.
16. Are there . . . . cakes in the cupboard?

(29) Look at the picture and write sentences as in the example:

1. Apples? *Are there any apples?*
   Yes, there are some apples.
2. Eggs? . . . .

3. Meat? . . . .

4. Butter? . . . .

5. Milk? . . . .

6. Tomatoes? . . . .

7. Oranges? . . . .

8. Beer? . . . .

9. Lemons? . . . .

(30) Now write what there is or there isn't in the fridge in your kitchen.

There is some meat. There . . . .

31 Look at the picture and write sentences as in the example:

1. Three children?

   ...Are there three children in the picture? ...
   ...No, there aren't. There are five children. ...

2. A birthday cake?

3. Three candles?

4. Two boys?

5. Two girls?

6. One bottle of Coca-Cola?

7. Five glasses?

8. One box?

9. One woman?

10. One man?

11. Five lollipops?

4. There is - are   a / some / any

32 **Fill in "There is", "There are", "Is there" or "Are there".**

1. *Are there.* any people on the bus?
2. .... any cheese in the sandwich?
3. .... some books in my bag.
4. .... some meat in the fridge.
5. .... any sugar in this tea?
6. .... some dogs in the garden.
7. .... a policeman in that car.
8. .... any matches in the matchbox?

9. .... any money in your pocket?
10. .... any horses in the field?
11. .... some Coca-Cola in that glass.
12. .... some letters on the table.
13. .... any water in the bottle?
14. .... any chairs in the room?
15. .... some paper on the desk.
16. .... a cat under the tree.

Guessing Game 8

The teacher chooses a leader from the class and tells him / her to imagine a fridge with 5 items inside (eg. milk, cheese, tomatoes, Coke, eggs). Then he / she divides the class into two groups and the groups in turn ask the leader questions about what is in the fridge. The group which finds most or all of the items within 10 questions wins.

Group A S1 :   Is there any milk in the fridge?
Leader :   Yes, there is some milk in the fridge.
Group B S1 :   Is there any beer in the fridge?
Leader :   No, there isn't any beer in the fridge.
Group A S2 :   Is there any cheese in the fridge?
Leader :   Yes, there is some cheese in the fridge.   etc.

Memory Game 9

The teacher divides the class into two groups and asks the students to look at the picture to ex 27 for 1 minute. Then the students close their books and the groups in turn try to remember as many items as possible. The group which finds most or all of the items wins.

Group A S1:   There's a slide in the picture.
Group B S1:   There's a ball in the picture.
Group A S2:   There's a tree in the picture.   etc.

5. Present Continuous

He **is reading** a newspaper. She **is bringing** the salad. The children **are fighting**. The cat **is eating** the chicken.

Affirmative		Negative		Interrogative
Long form	**Short form**	**Long form**	**Short form**	
I am working	I'm working	I am not working	I'm not working	Am I working?
You are working	You're working	You are not working	You aren't working	Are you working?
He is working	He's working	He is not working	He isn't working	Is he working?
She is working	She's working	She is not working	She isn't working	Is she working?
It is working	It's working	It is not working	It isn't working	Is it working?
We are working	We're working	We are not working	We aren't working	Are we working?
You are working	You're working	You are not working	You aren't working	Are you working?
They are working	They're working	They are not working	They aren't working	Are they working?

We use Present Continuous for temporary actions.

Look at the spelling of these verbs.

ru**n** - ru**nn**ing		work - wor**k**ing	open - ope**n**ing
di**g** - di**gg**ing	**BUT**	walk - wal**k**ing	listen - liste**n**ing
li**e** - l**y**ing		play - pla**y**ing	etc.

33 **Add -ing to the verbs.**

1. get .... *getting* ......
2. swim ....
3. stop ....

4. sit ....
5. watch ....
6. listen ....

7. drink ....
8. put ....
9. dig ....

5. Present Continuous

Look at the spelling of these verbs:

dance - dancing	have - having etc.

(34) Add -ing to the verbs.

1. live .... *living* ....
2. write ....
3. close ....

4. drive ....
5. smoke ....
6. come ....

7. ride ....
8. make ....
9. take ....

(35) Add -ing to the verbs.

1. sing . *singing*
2. read ....
3. open ....
4. eat ....
5. wash ....
6. count ....
7. sleep ....

8. go ....
9. win ....
10. show ....
11. jump ....
12. fly ....
13. give ....
14. feed ....

15. draw ....
16. score ....
17. bring ....
18. help ....
19. look ....
20. dream ....
21. enjoy ....

22. live ....
23. play ....
24. wake ....
25. move ....
26. visit ....
27. have ....
28. call ....

Time Expressions with Present Continuous		
now	at the moment	at present

Short Answers

Are you **sleeping?**	Yes, I am.
	No, I'm not.

Is	he she it	**sleeping?**	Yes, he she it is.
			No, he she it isn't.

Are they **sleeping?**	Yes, they are.
	No, they aren't.

(36) Write short answers.

1. Is the dog barking? Yes, ... *it is.* ....
2. Are the girls laughing? No, .. *they aren't.* ..
3. Are you doing your homework? No, ...
4. Is he driving a bus? Yes, ...
5. Are they watching television? Yes, ...
6. Is it raining outside? No, ...
7. Is she running? Yes, ...
8. Are they watering the flowers? Yes, ...
9. Is he putting on his coat? No, ...
10. Are they digging in the garden? No, ...
11. Are you writing a letter? Yes, ...
12. Are they listening to the radio? No, ...

28

(37) **Match the sentences with the pictures as in the example:**

Grandpa is sleeping.
Carol is listening to the radio.
They are eating.
The cat is jumping.

The women are cooking.
Sally is crying.
Jane and Bill are dancing.
Father is digging in the garden.

1. ... *Grandpa is sleeping.* ....

2. ....

3. ....

4. ....

5. ....

6. ....

7. ....

8. ....

(38) **Look at the pictures and write sentences as in the example:**

(cry)
Long form : ...*The baby is crying.*...
Short form : ...*It's crying.*...

1. (talk) ....

2. (sing) ....

3. (come) ....

4. (sit) ....

5. (wash the floor) ....

6. (drink Coke) ....

7. (open the window) ....

8. (write) ....

39 **Fill in the blanks with the correct form of the verb.**

It is Sunday morning and the family is on the beach. Mrs Fairfax 1) ....*is sleeping*..... (sleep) under a sun-umbrella.
Mr Fairfax 2) .... (read) a book.
Their two daughters 3) .... (swim) in the sea. Their son 4) .... (play) with a ball.

It is noon and the family is on the beach.

Look! The two girls 5) .... (run) towards the boy. Mrs Fairfax 6) .... (call) them. Mr Fairfax 7) .... (drink) some beer and he 8) .... (read) a book.

It is Sunday afternoon and their picnic is ready.
They 9) .... (enjoy) their picnic. They 10) .... (eat) sandwiches. John 11) .... (not/eat) his sandwich. He 12) .... (feed) the birds. They 13) .... (have) a wonderful day.

40 **Read the short texts above then ask and answer questions.**

1. ...*What is Mr Fairfax doing in picture 1? He is reading a book.*............
2. ....
   ....
3. ....
   ....
4. ....
   ....
5. ....
   ....

Look at the picture and write sentences as in the example:

1. Father is talking on the phone. ....*Wrong! Father isn't talking on the phone.* ...
.... *He's drinking beer.* ....

2. Grandpa is listening to music. ....
....

3. Father and mother are playing with the cat. ....
....

4. The boys are drinking beer. ....
....

5. Mother is sleeping. ....
....

6. Sue and Pam are watching TV. ....
....

7. Grandma is writing. ....
....

8. The cat is eating. ....
....

(42) Complete the sentences using the words in brackets.

What is my father doing in the living-room?
(read / book) ... *He is reading a book.* ....

1. What are Tom and Tina doing in the disco?
   (dance) ....
2. What are you doing?
   (listen/records) ....
3. What is the baby doing?
   (cry) ....
4. What is your sister doing in the bathroom?
   (have / a bath) ....
5. What are the boys doing in the park?
   (play / football) ....

(43) Ask questions which match the answers as in the example:

1. .... *Is mother cooking dinner?* ....   No, mother isn't cooking dinner.
2. ....   Yes, that man is cleaning the window.
3. ....   No, I am not swimming.
4. ....   Yes, we are going to the cinema tonight.
5. ....   No, it isn't raining today.
6. ....   Yes, the teacher is writing on the blackboard.
7. ....   Yes, the boys are swimming.
8. ....   No, you are not wearing a black shirt.
9. ....   No, I'm not washing my face.
10. ....   No, the dog isn't sleeping.

Game 10

Your teacher divides the class into two groups. Then, he /she asks a student (the leader) to come to the front of the class. The leader writes what the teacher is doing on a piece of paper (eg. He is writing). The students, by asking questions, try to guess what the teacher is doing.

Group A S1 :	Is he sleeping?	Leader :	No, he isn't.
Leader :	No, he isn't.	Group A S2 :	Is he writing?
Group B S1 :	Is he reading?	Leader :	Yes, he is.

Group A wins this time. Your teacher may choose another leader and you can play the game again.

Revision Exercises I

44 **Look at the picture and write what each person is doing.**

Mother (1) .. *is cooking* .. (cook). John (2) .... (read). Jane (3) ....
(eat) an apple. Father (4) .... (sleep). Grandfather (5) .... (watch)
TV. The dog (6) .... (lie) on the carpet. The girls (7) .... (play)
with their dolls.

Now look at the above picture and ask and answer.

1. (Mother / wear / red skirt?)   .. *Is Mother wearing a red skirt?* ....
   (blue skirt)   .. *No, she isn't. She is wearing a blue skirt.* ...

2. (John / write / a letter?) ....
   (read / book) ....

3. (Jane / eat / a banana?) ....
   (eat / apple) ....

4. (Grandfather / listen / radio?) ....
   (watch / TV) ....

5. (dog / sleep / on the chair?) ....
   (sleep / carpet) ....

6. (Father / watch TV?) ....

   (he / sleep) ....

45 Fill in "he", "she", "it", "we", "you" or "they".

1. You and John   ..you...............   5. eyes ....

2. Sally and I   ....   6. sister ....

3. Jane and Mary   ....   7. pen ....

4. book   ....   8. brother ....

46 Fill in the blanks and answer the questions as in the example :

1. ..Look at.. *it!* ....
   Is it a book?
   .*Yes, it is.*......

2. .Look at ....
   Is he a teacher?
   ....
   ....

3. Look at ....
   Are they boys?
   ....
   ....

4. Look at.............
   Are they rabbits?
   ....
   ....

5. Look at.............
   Is it a pen?
   ....
   ....

6. Look at ....
   Is she a policewoman?
   ....
   ....

7. Look at.............
   Are they cats?
   ....
   ....

8. Look at............
   Are they trees?
   ....
   ....

47 Ask and answer as in the example :

1. she / a doll?
   Has she got a doll?
   No, she hasn't.....
   She's got a book....

2. they / a picture?
   ....
   ....
   ....

3. the boy / a train?

. . . .

. . . .

. . . .

4. the cat / a mouse?

. . . .

. . . .

. . . .

5. the girl / an apple?

. . . .

. . . .

. . . .

6. the dog / a doll?

. . . .

. . . .

. . . .

48 Change to the plural.

1. My cat is black. *Our cats are black.*
2. This dog is white. . . . .
3. He is an old man. . . . .
4. This is a fat cat. . . . .
5. She is a good teacher. . . . .

6. I am tall. . . . .
7. This clown is funny. . . . .
8. This fox is brown. . . . .
9. He is a good doctor. . . . .
10. It is a book. . . . .

49 Fill in "This", "These" or "That".

1. . *This* . . is a basket.

2. . . . . is a shark.

3. . . . . are flowers.

4. .... is a picture.

50 **Underline the correct word.**

1. This book is (my / <u>mine</u>).
2. Mr Smith is (their / theirs) teacher.
3. This is (our / ours) house.
4. (My / Mine) dog is black and white.

5. The black skirt is (her / hers).
6. This is Pedro's book. It is (his / her).
7. This car is (their / theirs).
8. Dr Black is (her / hers) doctor.

51 **Write "There is" or "There are" as in the example:**

.There are. two pictures on the wall.

1. .... two beds in the bedroom.
2. .... a table in the bedroom.
3. .... a vase in the bedroom.
4. .... flowers in the vase.
5. .... a telephone in the bedroom.

6. .... four books in the bedroom.
7. .... two chairs in the bedroom.
8. .... a dog in the bedroom.
9. .... a cat in the bedroom.
10. .... two glasses on the table.

52 **Fill in "some" or "any".**

1. Are there .... *any* .... eggs in the fridge?
2. Is there .... cake left?
3. I have got .... pictures to show you.
4. Let's have .... ice-cream.
5. Is there .... bread on the table?
6. Let's buy .... cheese from the supermarket.

53 **Ask and answer as in the example :**

1. (write)
.*Can she write?*.
.. *Yes, she can*...

2. (play football)
....
....

3. (see)
....
....

4. (talk)
....
....

54 **Write sentences as in the example :**

1. He *is watering*.
...*the plants*...
....
....

2. They ....
....
....
....

3. The cat ....
....
....
....

4. The boy ....
....
....
....

5. They ....
....
....
....

6. He ....
....
....
....

Simple Present

Usually   **Today**

The monkey usually eats bananas.   But today it is eating an apple.

Affirmative	Negative		Interrogative
	Long form	**Short form**	
I work	I do not work	I don't work	Do I work?
You work	You do not work	You don't work	Do you work?
He works	He does not work	He doesn't work	Does he work?
She works	She does not work	She doesn't work	Does she work?
It works	It does not work	It doesn't work	Does it work?
We work	We do not work	We don't work	Do we work?
You work	You do not work	You don't work	Do you work?
They work	They do not work	They don't work	Do they work?

We use Simple Present for permanent or habitual actions.

Spelling

Verbs ending in ss, sh, ch, x, o ➡ es	Verbs ending in consonant + y ➡ ies
I wash - he washes I go - he goes	I cry - he cries BUT I play - he plays

Time Expressions with Simple Present			
Once a week	Every morning	Always	Never
Twice a week	Every year	Sometimes	At noon
Every day	Usually	Seldom	In the evening etc.

6. Simple Present

(55) **Write the third person singular.**

1. I teach - He .. *teaches.* ..
2. We study - He ....
3. You cook - She ....

4. They fly - It ....
5. I clean - She ....
6. I buy - He ....

7. You like - He ....
8. I do - She ....
9. We walk - He ....

(56) **Complete the sentences as in the example:**

Long Form		Short Form	
1. She .. *does not* ..speak Italian.		She .. *doesn't* ....speak Italian.	
2. They ....go to school.		They ....go to school.	
3. We ....swim very well.		We ....swim very well.	
4. He ....watch TV every day.		He ....watch TV every day.	
5. You ....live in England.		You ....live in England.	

(57) **Write what these people "do" or "don't do".**

	study hard	ride a bicycle	swim very well	listen to the radio
Penny	✔		✔	
Bob		✔	✔	✔
Don & Alice		✔		✔
You				

1. Penny *studies hard and swims very well but she doesn't ride a bicycle or listen* ..
   ..... *to the radio.* ....

2. Bob ....
   ....

3. Don and Alice ....
   ....

4. I ....
   ....

(58) **Fill in the blanks with the verbs from the box below:**

> be - love - clean - have - meet - go - sleep - teach - learn - come

Mary (1) ... *is* ...... a teacher. She (2) .... French. The children
(3) .... her and they (4) .... a lot from her. Mary
(5) .... home at 3:00 and (6) .... lunch. Then she
(7) .... for an hour. In the afternoon she (8) .... shopping or she
(9) .... her house. Sometimes she (10) .... her aunt and
(11) .... tea with her. Every Sunday she (12) .... her friends.

Short Answers

Do	you they	work?	Yes,	I / we they	do.	No,	I / we they	don't.
Does	he / she it	work?	Yes,	he / she it	does.	No,	he / she it	doesn't.

(59) **Complete the questions, then answer them as in the example:**

1. ... *Do* .... the girls like football? No, ... *they don't.* ....
2. .... Jim eat hamburgers? Yes, ...
3. .... you go to school? Yes, ...
4. .... she drink lemonade? No, ...
5. .... he help his mother? No, ...
6. .... they walk to school? Yes, ...
7. .... fish live in the water? Yes, ...
8. .... your dog sleep in your bedroom? No, ...
9. .... you like bananas? No, ...
10. .... Ann and Mary visit their grandparents? Yes, ...

(60) **Write sentences as in the example:**

1. Beth eats oranges. (bananas) .... *She doesn't eat bananas.* ....
2. Paul likes walking. (running) ....
3. They usually go to a disco. (bar) ....
4. Peter works in his office. (bedroom) ....
5. They drink water. (Coca-Cola) ....

6. Simple Present

Simple Present with Adverbs of Frequency		

She	sometimes always usually	comes early. travels by train.
He is	often seldom never	late.

It's Friday afternoon. Mrs West is cleaning the house. She **always cleans** the house on Friday afternoon.

61 Match the adverbs with the time expressions.

	always	usually	often	sometimes	seldom	never
1. every morning	✔					
2. once a year						
3. every day						
4. not at all						
5. once a month						
6. once every 10 years						
7. twice a week						
8. every Sunday						

62 Write what they usually do and what they're doing today.

Usually	Today

1. ....He usually sleeps in his bed...   2. ..But today he is sleeping on the sofa..

3. . . . .   4. . . . .

42

5. ....

6. ....

7. ....

8. ....

6 3 **First write about Liz then about yourself.**

	always		usually		often		sometimes		seldom		never	
	Liz	You	Liz	You	Liz	You	Liz	You	Liz	You	Liz	You
wash / hair					✔							
help / mother			✔									
get up early											✔	
do / homework	✔											
go / to the cinema							✔					
cry									✔			
play / tennis					✔							

..Liz often washes her hair. She usually helps her mother. She ....

....

....

....

..I

....

....

....

6. Simple Present

64 Put the verbs in brackets into the Simple Present or Present Cont.

Today (1) .. *is* .... (be) Sunday. My sister (2) .... (paint) a picture at the moment. My brothers (3) .... (ride) their bicycles in the garden now. They (4).................... (wear) their new jackets. I often (5) .... (read) a magazine on Sundays, but today I (6).................... (write) a letter to my cousin, Anna. She often (7).................... (send) me letters. Anna (8) .... (want) to be a doctor. Sometimes my mother (9) .... (ask) me what I (10)............. (want) to be, but I (11) .... (not/know).

65 You sent a letter to Paula. This is her reply. Write the questions you asked her.

114, Park Lane,
Harrow,
Middlesex.
13th March, 1992.

Dear Sue,

Thanks for your letter. I work in a school. I am a teacher. I live in a big house with my parents and I have one sister. She is fifteen years old. I have also got a pet dog. Its name is Benny. I like reading and sometimes I like going to the cinema. I like music a lot. My favourite pop star is Madonna.
Please write soon.

Yours, Paula

1. ..*Where do you work?* ....
2. ....
3. ....
4. ....
5. ....
6. ....
7. ....
8. ....
9. ....
10. ....

66 **Put the verbs into the Simple Present or Present Continuous.**

It (1) .*is*.. (be) Saturday afternoon and my sister and I (2) .... (be) at my friend's party. Some children (3) .... (dance) in the sitting-room now. My friend (4) .... (open) a present at the moment. Two children (5) .... (eat) chocolate cake, and three children (6) .... (play) a game. I often (7) .... (go) to parties because I (8) .... (have) a lot of friends. But I (9) .... (not/go) to parties on Sundays because I always (10) .... (visit) my grandparents on Sundays.

6. Simple Present

67 Choose a time expression from the box for each sentence.

now - on Fridays - always - at the moment - every night

1. My father is listening to the radio ..... *at the moment.* ....
2. I ....have toast for breakfast.
3. We watch the 9 o'clock news ....
4. My brother is doing his homework ....
5. My mother goes to the supermarket ....
6. I read a book or a magazine in bed ....
7. My grandmother ....sends me a birthday present.
8. My brother is playing football ....
9. At school we have our history lesson ....
10. My father ....buys a newspaper from the shop near his office.

68 Put the verbs into the Present Continuous or Simple Present.

1. Listen! The birds ... *are singing* ... (sing) in the garden!
2. I often .... (buy) fruit from the greengrocer's.
3. My mother .... (drink) tea now.
4. Look at Tom and Jim! They .... (walk) up the hill.
5. That man .... (laugh) at the moment.
6. The cat .... (play) with a ball now.
7. We always .... (wear) warm clothes in winter.
8. He often .... (eat) a sandwich at lunchtime.

69 Choose the correct item.

1. She .. *drinks* .. milk every morning.
A) drinks   B) is drinking   C) drink

2. We .... to the park now.
A) goes   B) are going   C) go

3. The woman .... shopping now.
A) goes   B) is going   C) go

4. She often .... her red dress.
A) wears   B) is wearing   C) wear

5. Look! The cat .... up the tree.
A) climbs   B) is climbing   C) climb

6. John .... to school now.
A) walks   B) is walking   C) walk

7. My cat usually .... by the fire.
A) sleep   B) is sleeping   C) sleeps

8. I .... a letter at the moment.
A) write   B) am writing   C) is writing

9. They ..... in a restaurant every Sunday.
A) eats   B) are eating   C) eat

10. Father always .... the grass.
A) cuts   B) cut   C) is cutting

70 **Put the verbs into the Simple Present or Present Continuous.**

It's Sunday at Ann's house.

Helen: Where (1) ... *is* ... (be) David?

Ann: He (2) . . . . (clean) his bicycle. He usually (3) . . . . (play)

           basketball on Sundays, but today he (4) . . . . (not/want) to play

           basketball.

Helen: (5) . . . . (be) your father in the garden now?

Ann: Yes, he (6) . . . . (cut) the grass. He (7) . . . . (not/like)

           long grass. He often (8) . . . . (say) that he (9) . . . . (want)

           a perfect garden! I usually (10) . . . . (help) him, but now I

           (11) . . . . (learn) some French verbs.

Helen: Why?

Ann: Because I (12) . . . . (not/know) them and we always

           (13) . . . . (have) a test on Monday morning!

71 **Put the verbs into the Simple Present or Present Continuous.**

Sarah usually (1) . . . . *goes* . . . . (go) swimming every Saturday but this Saturday it

(2) . . . . (be) her birthday. She (3) . . . . (like) chocolate cake so her

sister (4) . . . . (make) one for her now. Her mother (5) . . . . (cook)

food at the moment and her father (6) . . . . (do) the shopping. Sarah

(7) . . . . (want) everything to be nice for her party. Now she and her brother

(8) . . . . (make) hats for the children. They always (9) . . . . (have)

a good time at parties. They (10) . . . . (sing) and (11) . . . . (dance)

a lot and (12) . . . . (play) their favourite games.

Guessing Game 11

Your teacher divides the class into two groups and chooses a leader. Your teacher whispers
into the leader's ear what he/she often does (e.g. Teacher: "I often drive a car."). The groups
in turn try to guess what the teacher often does by asking the leader questions.

Group A S1 : Does he often play tennis? | Leader :   No, he doesn't.
Leader :   No, he doesn't. | Group A S2 : Does he often drive a car?
Group B S1 : Does he often play the guitar? | Leader :   Yes, he does.

Group A gets 1 point. The group with the most points is the winner.

7. The Imperative

We use the Imperative when we tell one or more persons to do something.

 Match the following with the pictures:

Open the window, please!	Drink your milk!	Sit down, please!
Let's go into the shop!	Let's play in the garden!	Be quiet, please!
Please don't walk on the grass!	Don't wake up the baby!	Don't smoke in your bedroom!

8. Prepositions of Place

73 **Look at the picture and read the text. Then cover the text and try to answer the questions that follow it.**

The old man is sitting **beside** the old woman. The young man is sitting **opposite** them. They are all sitting **by** the fireplace. There is a picture **above** the fireplace and a vase with flowers **below** the picture. There is a pram **behind** the man. The baby **in** the pram is crying. The pram is **in front of** the woman. She is taking the baby **out of** its pram. A young woman is going **through** the door-way **into** the living-room. There is a small table **in** the room and **on** that table there is a goldfish bowl. There is a goldfish **in** the bowl. A cat is **near** the bowl. The cat is putting its paw **into** the bowl. A little girl is going **up** the stairs and a dog is coming **down** the stairs. A boy is sitting **at** his desk. He is doing his homework.

1. Where is the old man sitting? .... *Beside the old woman.* ....
2. Where is the young man sitting? ....
3. Where are they all sitting? ....
4. Where is the picture? ....
5. Where is the vase? ....
6. Where is the pram? ....
7. Where is the baby? ....
8. Where is the woman? ....
9. Where is she taking the baby? ....
10. Where is the young woman going? ....
11. Where is the goldfish? ....
12. Where is the cat? ....
13. Where is the cat putting its paw? ....
14. Where is the dog going? ....
15. Where is the little girl going? ....
16. Where is the boy sitting? ....

(74) Look at the picture and read the text. Then cover the text and try to answer the questions that follow it.

There is a boy **between** the two girls. There is a cat **under** the tree and a bird is flying **over** the cat's head. There are some birds **among** the leaves of the trees. A cyclist is going **along** the street and an old man is walking **across** the street.

1. Where is the boy? ..... *Between the two girls.* ....
2. Where is the cat? ....
3. Where is the bird? ....
4. Where are the birds? ....
5. Where is the cyclist going? ....
6. Where is the old man walking? ....

(75) Look at the picture and fill in: "in", "beside", "behind", "into", "out of", "under", "in front of" or "on".

Two boys are playing with a ball 1) ..*in*.. the swimming pool. The old lady is sitting 2) .... the pool. There is a man reading a book 3) .... her. There is a small round table 4) .... the man. There is some Coca-Cola 5) .... the table and a little dog 6) .... the table. A young woman is diving 7) .... the pool and an old man is coming 8) .... the pool.

76 Look at the picture and fill in: "across", "along", "in front of", "near", "out of", "opposite" or "between".

There are some cars parked 1) ...*along*... the street. Lots of people are waiting 2) .... the bank. A policeman is helping an old lady 3) .... the street. A woman is getting 4) .... a car which is parked 5) .... two motorbikes 6) .... the bank. There are some children standing 7) .... the car.

77 Look at the pictures and fill in: "through", "on", "above", "in", "beside", "over" or "into".

Sam is sick and he is lying 1) ..*in*... bed 2) .... hospital. His friends Sue and Tom are visiting him. Sue is sitting 3) .... the bed and Tom is standing 4) .... the bed. There is a picture 5) .... Sam's bed. Sam is putting his hands 6) .... his mouth because he is coughing. A nurse is coming 7) .... the door 8) .... the room. It's time for Tom and Sue to leave.

8. Prepositions of Place

 Look at the picture and fill in: "above", "behind", "over", "on", "under", "at", "out of", "near" or "down".

Tom is sitting 1) ..*on*....a rug 2) .... his bed. His mother is standing 3) .... the door shouting at him. His clothes are all 4) .... the bed. There are empty bottles of Coca-Cola 5) .... the table 6) .... his bed. His toys are 7) .... the floor 8) .... the chair and his books are 9) .... the bed. The poster 10) .... his bed is falling 11) .... His socks are hanging 12) .... the drawer. His room is a mess and his mother is very angry.

Game 12

Look at the picture of the living-room in exercise 73 page 49.

Your teacher will ask a student to come to the front of the class. He / she will be the leader of the game. The leader must put the cat somewhere in the living-room. (e.g. The cat is under the table). Then the teacher divides the class into two groups. The groups ask the leader questions in turn until they find the cat. The winning group is the one which finds out where the cat is.

Group A S1:	Is the cat on the sofa?
Leader:	No, it isn't.
Group B S1:	Is the cat behind the sofa?
Leader:	No, it isn't.
Group A S2:	Is the cat under the table?
Leader:	Yes, it is.

Group A wins. Now the teacher can choose another leader and you can play the game again.

9. Prepositions of Time

In the evening	At noon	On Friday

He does his homework **in the evening**.	They have lunch together **at noon**	She goes shopping **on Friday**

in	at	on
in the morning	at 8 o'clock	on Sundays
in the afternoon	at noon	on Monday
in the evening	at night	on Tuesday (days) etc
in November (months)	at midnight	on October 4th (dates)
in summer (seasons)	at Easter	on Sunday afternoon
in 1992 (years)	at Christmas	

(79) Fill in "at", "in" or "on" as in the example:

1. ..*on*..... Saturday.
2. .... July.
3. .... 1984.
4. .... March 25th.
5. .... Friday.
6. .... summer.
7. .... the morning.

8. .... 9 o'clock.
9. .... Christmas.
10. .... September 28th.
11. .... 1991.
12. .... August 29th.
13. ..... Thursday afternoon.
14. .... the evening.

15. .... autumn.
16. .... half past two.
17. ...... Monday morning.
18. .... Easter.
19. .... 10 o'clock.
20. .... winter.
21. .... noon.

(80) Fill in "at", "in" or "on" as in the example:

1. ..*in*.... December.
2. .... midnight.
3. .... Wednesday evening.
4. .... April.
5. .... April 2nd.

6. .... a quarter past six.
7. .... noon.
8. .... 1982.
9. .... spring.
10. .... night.

11. .... February 8th.
12. .... Saturday night.
13. .... 1964.
14. .... Monday.
15. .... June 26th.

81 **Fill in the blanks with "in", "at" or "on" as in the example:**

1. We always go on holiday ...*in*...... summer.
2. My mother usually goes shopping .... Friday morning.
3. I always do my homework .... the evening.
4. The circus usually comes to our town .... spring.
5. Sophia's birthday is .... May 16th.
6. I usually get up .... seven o'clock.
7. My favourite television programme begins .... 6:30 .... the evening.
8. Sometimes it snows .... winter.
9. My friend's birthday is .... June.
10. Some birds and animals come out .... night.

82 **Choose the correct answer.**

1. My lesson starts ..*at*.. five o'clock.
    A) on .   B) at   C) in
2. My father usually buys a newspaper
   .... the morning.
    A) on   B) at   C) in
3. We wear warm clothes ......winter.
    A) on   B) at   C) in
4. We get presents ......Christmas.
    A) on   B) at   C) in

5. I usually visit my grandparents ....
    Sunday afternoon.
    A) on   B) at   C) in
6. John's birthday is .... August 16th.
    A) on   B) at   C) in
7. The film finishes .... 9:30.
    A) on   B) at   C) in
8. The supermarket is closed ......Sunday.
    A) on   B) at   C) in

Game 13

Your teacher will divide the class into two groups. Then he / she will say expressions of time without their prepositions. The groups in turn should complete the missing prepositions. Each correct answer gets one point. The group with the most points wins.

Teacher:	the afternoon	Group A S2:	in 1992
Group A S1:	in the afternoon	Teacher:	Christmas
Teacher:	night	Group B S2:	in Christmas
Group B S1:	at night	Teacher:	Wrong! at Christmas.
Teacher:	1992		Group B doesn't get a point.

10. How much / How many

Uncountable Nouns

How much?

How much cheese have I got?

Countable (Plural) Nouns

How many?

How many eggs have I got?

83 **Write the words from the box in the correct column.**

bread	lemon	water	woman	cheese	sugar	meat	beer	wine	room
bottle	boy	money	table	dog	glass	girl	tea	car	milk

Uncountable		Countable	
... bread	....	... bottle	....
....	....	....	....
....	....	....	....
....	....	....	....
....	....	....	....

84 **Write questions as in the example :**

1. sugar? .... *How much sugar have you got?* ....

2. dresses? ....

3. lemonade? ....

4. oranges? ....

5. meat? ....

6. chairs? ....

7. glasses? ....

8. cheese? ....

9. cats? ....

10. shirts? ....

11. jam? ....

12. books? ....

(85) **Ask and answer as in the example:**

1. *. How many apples are there? .*
   . Not many. .

2. ....

3. ....

4. ....

5. ....

6. ....

7. ....

8. ....

9. ....

10. ....

86 **Fill in "How much" or "How many".**

1. *How many* trees can you see?
2. .... money have you got?
3. .... eggs are there in the fridge?
4. .... biscuits have you got?
5. .... milk do you want?
6. .... bread do you want?
7. .... boys are in your class?
8. .... glasses are on the table?
9. .... butter is there on the plate?
10. .... books have you got?

11. .... dolls has the girl got?
12. .... balls have you got?
13. .... sandwiches do you want?
14. .... flowers are in the vase?
15. .... beer is there in the bottle?
16. .... pens are there in your bag?
17. .... tea is there in the bag?
18. .... hats have you got?
19. .... wine is there in the bottle?
20. .... meat is there in the fridge?

87 **Ask and answer as in the examples:**

1. ...*How much* ...... sugar is there? ...... *1 kilo.* ....
2. ...*How many* ...... oranges are there? ..*3 oranges.* ....
3. .... bread is there? ....
4. .... meat is there? ....
5. .... bananas are there? ....
6. .... coffee is there? ....
7. .... tomatoes are there? ....
8. .... biscuits are there? ....
9. .... milk is there? ....
10. .... potatoes are there? ....

Game 14

The teacher divides the class into two groups. Then he / she says nouns and the groups in turn add "how much" or "how many". Each correct answer gets 1 point. The group with the most points is the winner.

Teacher :	cheese		Teacher :	water
Group A S1 :	how much cheese?		Group A S2 :	how many water?
Teacher :	eggs		Teacher :	Wrong! "How much water?"
Group B S1 :	how many eggs?			Group A doesn't get a point.

Revision Exercises II

 88 **Fill in the blanks putting the verbs into their correct form:**

read	go	play	eat	want	come	be	like	work

John (1) ...*works*...in a bank. He (2) .... his job because it (3) .... very interesting. Many people (4) .... to the bank when they (5) .... money. When he (6) ... . home at night he (7) .... his dinner and (8) .... with his two children. Before they (9) .... to bed he (10) .... them a story.

89 **Fill in the blanks with one of the words from the box below:**

at the moment	usually	seldom	never

1. I ...*never*.............. go to school on Christmas Day.
2. I am writing a letter ....
3. I .... eat meat; I don't like it very much.
4. I .... go to church on Sundays.

90 **Put the verbs into the Simple Present or Present Continuous.**

1. The children ..*are playing* ..(play) outside now.
2. He sometimes .... (go) to church.
3. I .... (do) my homework at the moment.
4. I........................... (read) the newspaper every morning.
5. I .... (eat) my dinner now.

6. She usually . . . . (read) a book in the evening.

7. We . . . . (go) to the disco tonight.

8. He . . . . (write) a letter to his penfriend every month.

9. My mother usually . . . . (cook) dinner in the evening.

10. She . . . . (travel) to work by train every day.

91 Choose the correct item.

1. She ..*eats*.. meat every day.
   A) is eating   B) eats   C) eat

2. The baby . . . . at the moment.
   A) is sleeping   B) sleeps   C) sleep

3. I . . . . to bed every night at 10.00 pm.
   A) am going   B) goes   C) go

4. Dad . . . . TV now.
   A) is watching   B) watches   C) watch

5. Mother always . . . . the dishes.
   A) is washing   B) washes   C) wash

6. Jane . . . . a book at the moment.
   A) is reading   B) reads   C) read

7. She . . . . very quickly. Look!
   A) is running   B) runs   C) run

8. I . . . . my homework every day.
   A) am doing   B) do   C) does

92 Fill in "in", "at" or "on".

1. I usually go to the park ..*on*.. Sundays.
2. We go skiing . . . . December.
3. I am going to Spain . . . . summer.
4. We don't go to school . . . . Easter.
5. I got up . . . . 8.00 am this morning.

6. Are you going to the disco . . . . Saturday?
7. We learn many things . . . . school.
8. I don't like getting up . . . . the morning.
9. I am going to the dentist . . . . . . Monday.
10. I go to bed . . . . 10 o'clock.

93 Fill in the third person singular.

1. I write - He ..*writes*..
2. I catch - He . . . .
3. I cry - He . . . .

4. I buy - He . . . .
5. I give - He . . . .
6. I kiss - He . . . .

7. I dance - He . . . .
8. I take - He . . . .
9. I go - He . . . .

94 Fill in "How much" or "How many".

1. ..*How many*. apples are there in the bag?
2. . . . . money have you got?
3. . . . . girls are there in your class?
4. . . . . milk is there?
5. . . . . records have you got?

6. . . . . butter do you want?
7. . . . . people can you see?
8. . . . . sugar do you want?
9. . . . . children can you see?
10. . . . . meat do you want?

95 **Fill in the correct preposition.**

under	between	behind	out of	at	on	in	into

The cat is sleeping 1) ...*in*....its basket. Dinner is 2) .... the table. Grandfather is sitting 3) .... the table. Peter is sitting 4) .... Sally and Grandfather. Father is looking 5) .... the window.The dog is playing with a ball 6) .... the chair. John is 7) .... the chair. Grandmother is coming 8) .... the room with some wine.

96 **Underline the correct word as in the example:**

1. Tina is (my, mine) sister.
2. This car is (her, his).
3. These are the children's shoes.They're (their, theirs).
4. These books are (your, yours).
5. That skirt is (her, hers).
6. (My, Mine) brother is tall.
7. This is Sue's bicycle. It's (her, hers) bicycle.
8. That is (your, yours) pen.
9. These are (our, ours) pencils.
10. This shirt is (her, his).

97 **Put the verbs in brackets into the Simple Present or Present Continuous.**

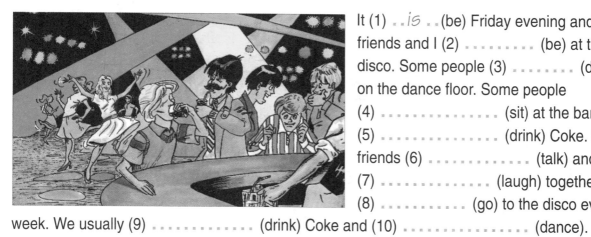

It (1) ..*is*.. (be) Friday evening and my friends and I (2) .... (be) at the disco. Some people (3) .... (dance) on the dance floor. Some people (4) .... (sit) at the bar and (5) .... (drink) Coke. My friends (6) .... (talk) and (7) .... (laugh) together. We (8) .... (go) to the disco every week. We usually (9) .... (drink) Coke and (10) .... (dance).

98 **Change to the plural.**

1. She has got a child. ....*They have got children.*...............
2. This is my car. ....
3. It is an ox. ....
4. That is a fox. ....
5. He is a singer. ....

99 **Fill in "some" or "any".**

1. Is there ......*any*.............. beer in the bottle?
2. There are .... biscuits in the tin.
3. There aren't .... pens on the desk.
4. There are .... flowers in the vase.
5. Are there .... cups in the cupboard?
6. There isn't .... cheese in the fridge.

100 **Fill in "There is" or "There are".**

1. ....*There are*.............. some bottles of Coke on the table.
2. .... some milk in the fridge.
3. .... a man at the door.
4. .... zebras in the zoo.
5. .... a box on the table.

11. Be going to

I am going to leave this job. I am going to be a famous star. I am going to be rich. I am going to ....

Miss Sheldan! Are you going to finish your work?

| I am you are he, she, it is we, you, they are | going to + verb |

Time Expressions with "Be going to"

tomorrow, tonight, next week / month / year

We use "be going to" for plans and intentions
or when there is evidence that something is going to happen in the future.

101 **Write sentences as in the example:**

1. (play/tennis) I .*am going to* ....*play tennis*.................

2. (fight) They ....

3. (sleep) We . . . .

4. (wash/the dishes) She . . . .

5. (open/his umbrella) He . . . .
. . . .

6. (post / a letter) He . . . .
. . . .

7. (feed/the dog) He . . . .
. . . .

8. (cut/some bread)She . . . .
. . . .

 Complete the sentences as in the example:

1. (dig/in the garden)
*They are . . . .
going to dig . . . . .
in the garden. . . .*

2. *They are . . . .
digging in the . .
garden. . . . .*

3. (listen/to the record)
. . . .
. . . .
. . . .

4. . . . .
. . . .
. . . .

5. (rain)
. . . .
. . . .
. . . .

6. . . . .
. . . .
. . . .

7. (make/a cake)

....
....
....

8. ....
....
....

103 Write questions and answers as in the example:

	teacher	doctor	singer	football player
Fred		✔		
Rod & Ben			✔	
Joan	✔			
Ted				✔
You				

1. Fred / singer? ... *Is Fred going to be a singer?* ....
   .. *No, he isn't. He isn't going to be a singer.* ....
   .. *He is going to be a doctor.* ....

2. Rod and Ben / teachers? ....
   ....
   ....

3. Joan / doctor? ....
   ....
   ....

4. Ted / singer? ....
   ....
   ....

5. You / teacher? ....
   ....
   ....

(104) Look at Julie's diary and write what her plans are for next week. Then write about your plans.

Monday: meet Jane
Tuesday: stay at home
Wednesday: clean the house
Thursday: buy new shoes
Friday: visit my grandmother
Saturday: go to the theatre
Sunday: have dinner with some friends

1. *Julie is going to meet Jane on Monday.*
2. ....
3. ....
4. ....
5. ....
6. ....
7. ....

1. I am going to ....
2. ....
3. ....
4. ....
5. ....
6. ....
7. ....

Mon: _____
Tues: _____
Wed: _____
Thur: _____
Fri: _____
Sat: _____
Sun: _____

Game 15

The teacher divides the class into two groups and chooses a leader. The leader thinks of five things he / she is going to do tomorrow. The groups in turn ask questions. Each correct guess gets 1 point. The group with the most correct guesses is the winner.

(List : dance - draw - do homework - go to the cinema - visit my friend).

Group A S1 :	Are you going to read?	Leader :	Yes, I am.
Leader :	No, I'm not.	Group A S2 :	Are you going to do your homework?
Group B S1 :	Are you going to draw?	Leader :	Yes, I am. etc.

12. Love / hate / like / don't like doing something

105 **Write about Tom, then write about you.**

	like		don't like		love		hate	
	Tom	You	Tom	You	Tom	You	Tom	You
go on holiday	✔							
get up early					✔			
clean room			✔					
go to the doctor's							✔	
read stories	✔							

1. Tom . . . *likes going on holiday.* . . . .
2. . . . .
3. . . . .
4. . . . .
5. . . . .
6. I . . . .
7. . . . .

8. ....
9. ....
10. ....

106 **Put the verbs in brackets into the - ing form.**

Sally and her family love
.. *going* .(go) to the park
in the summer. They like
(1) .... (have)
picnics and love
(2) .... (sit) on the
grass. Sally's mother hates
(3) .... (make)
sandwiches so her father
always makes them. Sally
and her brother love
(4) .... (play) with
a ball in the park. Sally's
mother likes (5) .... (lie) on the blanket and loves (6) .... (read) her favourite
magazines. Sally loves (7) .... (listen) to the birds singing in the trees and her
brother likes (8) .... (watch) the people in the park. Sally's family likes the park
because they love (9) .... (be) outdoors.

107 **Write questions and answers as in the example:**

1. the girls / eat chocolate.
   (like) .*Do the girls like eating chocolate?*
   (Yes, love) *Yes, they love eating chocolate.*

2. Polly / touch spiders.
   (like) ....
   (No, hate) ....

12. Love / hate / like / don't like doing something

3. the dog / have a bath.

(like) ....

(No, hate) ....

4. the children / watch TV.

(like) ....

(Yes, love) ....

5. Tom / do his homework.

(like) ....

(No, not like) ....

6. Sam / get up early.

(like) ....

(No, hate) ....

7. the children / go to the circus.

(like) ....

(Yes, like) ....

8. the baby / take medicine.

(like) ....

(No, hate) ....

9. Father / clean the car.

(like) ....

(No, not like) ....

10. they / drink beer.

(like) ....

(Yes, like) ....

(108) **Complete the sentences as in the example:**

	ride a bicycle	watch TV	play football	swim
Jane	✔			✔
Mike		✔	✔	
Rod & Ben	✔			✔
Jennifer		✔		✔
You				

1. Jane *likes riding a bicycle and swimming. She doesn't like watching TV or playing football.*

2. Mike ....

   ....

3. Rod and Ben ....

   ....

4. Jennifer ....

   ....

5. I ....

   ....

Game 16

The teacher divides the class into two groups. Each group makes up sentences in turn. One student from group A starts saying what he/she likes. The next student from group B says what the previous student likes and adds what he/she likes and so on. Each correct sentence gets 1 point. The group with the most points is the winner.

Example : Group A S1 :   I like fishing.
          Group B S1 :   I like fishing and reading.
          Group A S2 :   I like fishing, reading and dancing.
          Group B S2 :   I like fishing, reading, dancing and singing.
          Group A S3 :   (silence)
          Group A doesn't get a point.

13. Must / Mustn't

Must expresses obligation or necessity. **Mustn't** expresses prohibition.

109 **Mr Welsh has got a cold and is coughing a lot. The doctor is telling him what he must or mustn't do.**

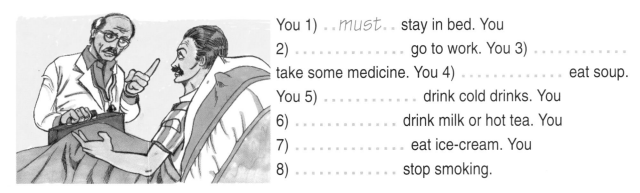

You 1) ..*must*.. stay in bed. You
2) .... go to work. You 3) ....
take some medicine. You 4) .... eat soup.
You 5) .... drink cold drinks. You
6) .... drink milk or hot tea. You
7) .... eat ice-cream. You
8) .... stop smoking.

110 **Mother is telling her son what he must or mustn't do.**

1. You .... *must* ..... do your homework.
2. You .... be late for school.
3. You .... talk in class.
4. You .... tidy your room.
5. You .... go to bed late.
6. You .... get up early.

(111) Match the sentences with the pictures .

You mustn't smoke in here.   You mustn't swim here.   You must drive slowly.
You mustn't walk on the grass.   You mustn't park here.   You must stop here.

1. *You must drive slowly.*   2. ....   3. ....

4. ....   5. ....   6. ....

 (112) Mr Brown has problems with his heart. The doctor is telling him what he must or mustn't do.

You 1) . *must* . lose weight. You 2) .... eat sweets. You 3) .... eat so much. You 4) .... eat vegetables. You 5) .... smoke. You 6) .... work too hard. You 7) .... walk a lot. You 8) .... take some exercise. You 9) .... drink beer or wine. You 10) .... go to bed early. You 11) .... take some medicine. You 12) .... go out in cold weather.

Game 17

Your teacher will divide the class into two groups. Then he /she will say "must" or "mustn't" and the groups in turn make up sentences. Each correct sentence gets 1 point. The group with the most points is the winner.

Teacher :	must		Group A S2 :	You mustn't be late.
Group A S1 :	You must drive carefully.		Teacher :	must
Teacher :	must		Group B S2 :	You must tell lies.
Group B S1 :	You must be polite.		Teacher :	Wrong! You must tell the truth.
Teacher :	mustn't			Group B doesn't get a point.

14. Past Tense (Was – Were)

Today   **Then**

Affirmative	Negative		Interrogative
	Long form	**Short form**	
I was	I was not	I wasn't	Was I?
You were	You were not	You weren't	Were you?
He was	He was not	He wasn't	Was he?
She was	She was not	She wasn't	Was she?
It was	It was not	It wasn't	Was it?
We were	We were not	We weren't	Were we?
You were	You were not	You weren't	Were you?
They were	They were not	They weren't	Were they?

We use past tense for actions which happened at a definite time in the past.

Past tense with time expressions.

yesterday	last month	two weeks ago	two days ago
last week	last year	two months ago	then etc.

113 **Fill in "is", "are", "was" or "were".**

1. The birds are in the cage.

The birds . *were* . in the cage but they
..... *are* .... out of the cage now.

2. The goldfish is in the bowl.

The goldfish .... in the bowl
but it .... in the cat's mouth now.

3. The children are in the class.

The children .... in the class
but they .... at home now.

4. The cat is on the chair.

The cat .... on the chair but
it .... under the table now.

14. Past Tense (Was - Were)

114 Fill in the blanks with "am", "is", "are", "was" or "were".

1. It .. *is* ... Monday today. Jim and Mary
   .. *are* ... at work. It .. *was* ...
   Sunday yesterday and they .. *were*... at home.

2. It .... midnight. The children ....
   in bed. They .... in the living-room
   three hours ago.

3. It .... 12 noon and she .... in
   the kitchen. She .... in the garden
   two hours ago.

4. It .... Saturday today. The girls ....
   at their grandmother's. They ....
   at the zoo last Saturday.

115 Look at ex. 114 then ask and answer questions as in the example:

1. Jim and Mary / at work / Sunday?
   .... *Were Jim and Mary at work on Sunday?* ....
   .... *No, they weren't. They were at home.* ....

2. the children / in bed / three hours ago?

3. she / in the kitchen / two hours ago?

4. the girls / at their grandmother's / last Saturday?

74

116 Fill in "There is" or "There are".

1) *There is* a man and a woman in the living-room. 2) .... two children. 3) .... a TV. 4) .... two chairs and 5) .... two armchairs. 6) .... a table in front of the fireplace and 7) .... some books on it. 8) .... a vase with flowers on the table too. 9) .... a carpet on the floor. 10) .... two pictures on the wall. 11) .... a small round table near the window and 12) .... a telephone on it.

117 Look at ex. 116 first. Then look at the picture and write what "there was / were" in the living-room.

There was a man and a woman in the living-room.

(118) Fill in the blanks with "was", "am", "is", "are" or "were".

Today .*is* .Christmas Day and my family and I (1) . . . . at home. It
(2) . . . . Christmas Eve yesterday and we (3) . . . . in town
shopping for presents. It (4) . . . . not cold yesterday but today it (5) . . . .
very cold and it (6) . . . . snowing outside. We (7) . . . . not cold because there
(8) . . . . a big fire in the living-room and we (9) . . . . all nice and warm. I like
Christmas and I (10) . . . . very happy today.

Game 18

The teacher divides the class into two groups and chooses a leader. The leader writes on a
piece of paper where he/she was last night (e.g. I was at my grandmother's). The groups in
turn ask 5 questions each. The group that finds out where he/she was is the winner. If the
groups fail to guess correctly, the game is a draw.

Group A S1 :	Were you at home?		Group A S2 :	Were you at the cinema?
Leader :	No, I wasn't.		Leader :	No, I wasn't.
Group B S1 :	Were you at work?		Group B S2 :	Were you at your grandmother's?
Leader :	No, I wasn't.		Leader :	Yes, I was.

Group B is the winner. The teacher chooses another leader and you can play the game again.

15. Past Tense (Had)

You look tired today Jane, why?

Well, I had my birthday party last night. We all had fun but I had a lot of work to do after the party.

Affirmative	Negative		Interrogative
	Long form	**Short form**	
I had	I did not have	I didn't have	Did I have?
You had	You did not have	You didn't have	Did you have?
He had	He did not have	He didn't have	Did he have?
She had	She did not have	She didn't have	Did she have?
It had	It did not have	It didn't have	Did it have?
We had	We did not have	We didn't have	Did we have?
You had	You did not have	You didn't have	Did you have?
They had	They did not have	They didn't have	Did they have?

(119) Complete the sentences as in the example:

1. (a banana)

..He has got a..
..banana........

2.

..He had a......
..banana.......

3. (a new car)

....
....

4.

....
....

77

5. (an umbrella)

6.

7. (a vase)

8.

120 **They went on a picnic last Sunday. Write what each one of them had.**

	apples	oranges	pears	sandwiches	Coke	beer
Jean	3		2	2	1	
Mike		2		3		2
Don & Jim	2		3	2	3	
Helen	1	3			2	1
Carol		1	2	2	2	

1. Jean ..*had three apples, two pears, two sandwiches and one bottle of* ...
   ..*Coke. She didn't have any oranges or beer.*

2. Mike

3. Don and Jim

4. Helen

5. Carol

| Short Answers | Yes, | I / you / he / she / it we / you / they | did. | No, | I / you / he / she / it we / you / they | didn't. |

121 **Look at ex. 120. Then ask and answer as in the example:**

1. (Jean / beer?) .. *Did Jean have any beer? No, she didn't.* ....
2. (Jean / pears?) ....
3. (Mike / oranges?) ....
4. (Mike / beer?) ....
5. (Mike / apples?) ....
6. (Don and Jim / beer?) ....
7. (Don and Jim / sandwiches?) ....
8. (Carol / pears?) ....

Game 19

The teacher divides the class into two groups and chooses a leader. The leader makes a list of the things he / she had for breakfast. The groups in turn try to guess what he / she had for breakfast. Each group can ask five questions. Each correct guess gets 1 point. The group which guesses most or all the things is the winner.

Leader: eggs, jam, toast, tomato juice, cake, eggs

Group A S1 :	Did you have bacon for breakfast?	Leader :	Yes, I did.	
Leader :	No, I didn't.	Group A S2 :	Did you have eggs for breakfast?	
Group B S1 :	Did you have toast for breakfast?	Leader :	Yes, I did. etc.	

Revision Exercises III

122 **Fill in "must" or "mustn't".**

1. He is late. He .. *must* .. run to school.
2. He is sick. He .... go to school.
3. She has a cold. She .... take some medicine.
4. Your hands are dirty. You .... wash them.

Revision Exercises III

(123) Fill in "How much" or "How many".

1. ... *How much* ... money have you got?
2. .... days are there in a week?
3. .... butter is there on the plate?
4. .... books have you got?

(124) Complete the chart and then write sentences.

	like		don't like		love		hate	
	Your friend	You	Your friend	You	Your friend	You	Your friend	You
Go to school			✔					
Go to the dentist's							✔	
Eat sweets					✔			
Cut the grass			✔					
Go to bed late	✔							

1. ... *My friend doesn't like going to school.* ....
2. ....
3. ....
4. ....
5. ....
6. I ....
7. ....
8. ....
9. ....
10. ....

(125) Change to the plural as in the example:

It is a record. ... *They are records.* ...

1. He is a policeman. ....
2. I am English. ....
3. She is a woman. ....

4. This is a box. ....
5. She is a housewife. ....
6. It is a foot. ....
7. That is a goose. ....

126 **Match the sentences with the pictures as in the example:**

You mustn't talk in the library.
You must have a bath.

You mustn't eat or drink in the classroom.
You must brush your teeth after meals.

1. ...*You must brush your teeth.*
...*after meals.*...............

2. ....

3. ....
....

4. ....
....

127 **Ask and answer the questions as in the example:**

1. Sam / in London / last week?

..*Was Sam in London last week?*
..*No, he wasn't. He was in Paris.*.

2. Jim and Tom / at work / yesterday?

....
....

3. the girls / at the zoo / yesterday?

....
....

4. you and your friend / at the cinema / last night?

....
....

Revision Exercises III

128 **Ask questions and answer with short answers as in the example:**

1. John / dog?　　　　　2. boy / bike?　　　　　3. children / television?

Has John got a dog?　......................................　......................................
Yes, he has...........　......................................　......................................

129 **Fill in the right word from the list as in the example:**

mine	yours	his	hers	its	ours	our	theirs	their

1. The cat is .. *hers*......... . (Sally)
2. The car is .... (You and Helen)
3. These books are .... (Donna and I)
4. Are those cards .... ? (Debbie and Jane)
5. It is .... food. (dog)
6. That red car is .... (Jane)
7. Those flowers are .... (Mother)
8. When is .... birthday? (Father)
9. .... car is black. (Jack and Joan)
10. That bag is .... (I)

130 **Put the verbs into the Present Continuous or Simple Present.**

1. Mary .. *is washing* .... (wash) her hair at the moment.
2. My brothers .... (play) basketball now.
3. My father .... (work) in a bank.
4. My mother always .... (go) to the supermarket on Fridays.
5. Julia .... (paint) a picture at the moment.
6. Michael .... (not/live) in Athens.
7. Lucy .... (wear) her new shoes now.
8. Trevor .... (not/like) potatoes.
9. My father always .... (drive) to work.
10. We .... (do) our homework at the moment.

(131) Fill in "some" or "any".

1. There are ... *some* .... people in the shop.
2. Is there .... milk in that cup?
3. There is .... cheese in this sandwich.
4. Are there .... pencils on the table?
5. There isn't .... bread here.
6. There are .... pens on his desk.
7. Are there .... letters for me?
8. There isn't .... meat on the plate.
9. There are .... elephants in the zoo.
10. Are there .... cats in the garden?
11. Is there .... water in the bottle?
12. There is .... coffee in the cup.

(132) Write the words in the correct column as in the examples:

box	money	pencil	star	water	circus	bag	book
cheese	tomato	dress	meat	bread	milk	tea	pen

Countable Nouns		Uncountable Nouns	
Box, ...	....	*Cheese,*	....
....	....	....	....
....	....	....	....
....	....	....	....

(133) Fill in with "a", "an" or "some".

1. ... *a* .... teacher
2. ....egg
3. ....tea
4. ....umbrella
5. ....shirt
6. ....money
7. ....spoon

8. ....jam
9. ....lemonade
10. ....meat
11. ....bottle of wine
12. ....coffee
13. ....loaf of bread
14. ....bread

15. ....sugar
16. ....bowl of sugar
17. ....milk
18. ....carton of milk
19. ....glass of water
20. ....water
21. ....octopus

(134) **Fill in "There is", "There are", "Is there" or "Are there".**

1. .. *There are* . some eggs in the basket.
2. .... some butter in the fridge.
3. .... any knives on the table?
4. .... any popcorn in the box?
5. .... any jam in this sandwich?
6. .... some birds in the tree.
7. .... trees in the garden?
8. .... any money in that box?
9. .... any mice under the bed?
10. .... any wine in the bottle?
11. .... any beer in the glass?
12. .... any horses in the field?
13. .... monkeys in the zoo?
14. .... apples in the fridge.
15. .... some flowers in the vase.
16. .... any milk in the fridge?

(135) **Fill in "Am", "Is", "Are", "Do" or "Does".**

1. . *Do* ... you want to come with us?
2. .... she like her new house?
3. .... he ill?
4. .... they going to be at the party?
5. .... he like your new dress?
6. .... she work hard?
7. .... you still angry with me?
8. .... he finish work at 6 pm?
9. .... you coming to the party tonight?
10. .... I late again?

(136) **Ask and answer the questions as in the examples:**

1. Look at .. *it!* ......
.. *Is it* ... a bird?
. *Yes it is.* ....
....

2. Look at .. *them!* .
Are they . apples?
No, they aren't. .
They are trees. .

3. Look at ....!
...... a helicopter?
....
....

4. Look at ....!
.... bicycles?
....
....

5. Look at ....!
.... a man?
....
....

6. Look at ....!
.... a church?
....
....

137 **Write the -ing form for these verbs.**

1. help *. helping ....*   4. make ....   7. drive ....
2. look ....   5. walk ....   8. write ....
3. buy ....   6. laugh ....   9. hit ....

138 **Look at the picture and fill in the the correct preposition.**

There is a plant 1) .....*on*........ the table. There is a telephone 2) .... the book and the plant. There is a picture 3) .... the table. There is a cat 4) .... the table. There is a mat 5) .... the door. 6) .... the mat there are some letters. There is a shopping bag 7) .... the chair. There is a newspaper 8) .... the shopping bag. 9) .... the chair there is an umbrella. There is a boy 10) .... the door.

139 **Put the verbs in the "Simple Present" or "Present Continuous".**

Kate: Hello Peter! What (1) ... *are you doing* ... (you/do) right now?
Peter: I (2) .... (play) with my dog Rex.
Kate: (3) .... (you/want) to take Rex for a walk on the beach?
Peter: No, Rex (4) .... (not/like) the sea!
Kate: (5) .... (he/like) the park?
Peter: Yes, he does. Let's go there now!

(140) Put the verbs into the "Simple Present" or "Present Continuous".

I (1) .. *am watching* .. (watch) television now. I (2) .... (not / know) the name of the television programme. It (3) .... (finish) at seven o'clock. My sister (4) ... . (listen) to the radio now in the kitchen. She (5) .... (make) a cake. She (6) .... (not / like) television. She (7) .... (read) a lot of books. She (8) .... (go) to the library every Saturday, and (9) .... (borrow) four or five books. I (10) .... (not / know) how many books she (11) .... (have) in her room.

(141) Fill in "in", "at" or "on".

1. ..*on*.. Monday
2. .... May
3. .... summer
4. .... 8 o'clock
5. .... Christmas

6. .... noon
7. .... the morning
8. 1995
9. .... Sunday morning
10. .... the afternoon

11. .... August
12. .... midnight
13. .... 10 o'clock
14. .... August 2nd
15. .... Monday afternoon

(142) Complete the sentences using "be going to" or Present Continuous.

1. (eat)
.*They are going.*
..*to eat.*........
....

2.
.*They are eating.*
....
....

3. (have / a bath)
....
....
....

4.
....
....
....

5. (wash / his car)
....
....
....

6.
....
....
....

16. Simple Past (Regular Verbs)

Did you tidy your room Ben?

No, I didn't tidy it, mum.

I helped Helen make a cake.

We form the past tense of regular verbs by adding -ed.

Regular verbs

Affirmative	Negative		Interrogative
	Long form	**Short form**	
I walked	I did not walk	I didn't walk	Did I walk?
You walked	You did not walk	You didn't walk	Did you walk?
He walked	He did not walk	He didn't walk	Did he walk?
She walked	She did not walk	She didn't walk	Did she walk?
It walked	It did not walk	It didn't walk	Did it walk?
We walked	We did not walk	We didn't walk	Did we walk?
You walked	You did not walk	You didn't walk	Did you walk?
They walked	They did not walk	They didn't walk	Did they walk?

Spelling

love - loved   study - studied   stop - stopped   walk - walked
like - liked   stay - stayed   prefer - preferred listen - listened

143 **Write the Simple Past of the following verbs.**

1. watch ..*watched*.
2. clean ....
3. stop ....
4. arrive ....
5. return ....
6. cook ....

7. walk ....
8. visit ....
9. work ....
10. look ....
11. like ....
12. iron ....

13. play ....
14. study ....
15. love ....
16. open ....
17. start ....
18. water ....

19. climb ....
20. stay ....
21. call ....
22. kiss ....
23. tidy ....
24. wash ....

16. Simple Past (Regular Verbs)

**We use the Past tense for actions
which happened in the past at a definite time.**

(144) **Helen usually does the housework but yesterday Helen was ill,
so Peter did the housework. Write sentences as in the example:**

Usually   **Yesterday**

1. clean/the house

Helen usually ....
cleans the house ....
but yesterday Peter ..
cleaned the house. ...

2. wash/the dishes

3. cook/dinner

4. iron/the clothes

5. walk/the dog

145 **Write sentences as in the example:**

	clean the house	water the flowers	watch TV	listen to the radio
Susan	✔	✔		
Simon			✔	✔
Mr & Mrs Hill	✔		✔	
Helen		✔	✔	
You				

1. Susan .. *cleaned the house and watered the flowers yesterday.* ....
   ...... *She didn't watch TV or listen to the radio.* ....

2. Simon ....
   ....

3. Mr and Mrs Hill ....
   ....

4. Helen ....
   ....

5. I ....
   ....

Short Answers	Yes,	I / you / he / she / it we / you / they	did.	No,	I / you / he / she / it we / you / they	didn't.

146 **Look again at exercise 145 then ask and answer.**

1. Susan/listen to the radio? *Did Susan listen to the radio yesterday? No, she didn't.*
2. Susan/watch TV? ....
3. Simon/clean the house? ....
4. Simon/water the flowers? ....
5. Simon/watch TV? ....
6. Mr and Mrs Hill/clean the house? ....
7. Mr and Mrs Hill/listen to the radio? ....
8. Mr and Mrs Hill/water the flowers? ....

16. Simple Past (Regular Verbs)

147 Put the verbs into the Simple Past.

Yesterday my family and I
....*visited*.... (visit) my
grandparents. My mother
(1) .... (help) my
grandmother with the
housework. My father
(2) .... (clean) the
windows outside. My brother
and I (3) .... (watch)
cartoons on television and later
we (4) .... (play)
outside in the garden.

We (5) .... (climb) the tree to our tree-house. We (6) .... (stay) there all afternoon. Then our mother (7) .... (call) us because it was time to go home. Our grandparents (8) .... (kiss) us goodbye and we (9) .... (return) home. We (10) .... (arrive) home at 8 o'clock. Father (11) .... (look) for the key, (12) .... (open) our front door and we all (13) .... (walk) inside.

148 Fill in with the Simple Past.

Yesterday my sister and I
(1) .... *helped* .... (help) our
mother in the house. First we
(2) .... (clean)
our rooms and then we
(3) .... (wash)
our clothes. After that we
(4) .... (cook)
some spaghetti. The spaghetti
(5) .... (not / be)
very nice, but our mother
(6) .... (be)
happy to eat it. Then I

(7) .... (have) a bath and my sister and I (8) .... (watch) TV.

17. Simple Past (Irregular Verbs)

Affirmative	Negative		Interrogative
	Long form	**Short form**	
I went	I did not go	I didn't go	Did I go?
You went	You did not go	You didn't go	Did you go?
He went	He did not go	He didn't go	Did he go?
She went	She did not go	She didn't go	Did she go?
It went	It did not go	It didn't go	Did it go?
We went	We did not go	We didn't go	Did we go?
You went	You did not go	You didn't go	Did you go?
They went	They did not go	They didn't go	Did they go?

149 **Fill in the blanks.**

Present	Past	Present	Past
1. is / are	..*was / were*..	14. meet	....
2. ..*break*...	broke	15. put	....
3. buy	....	16. read	....
4. come	....	17.	rode
5. cut	....	18.	ran
6.	cost	19. see	....
7. drink	....	20. sit	....
8. drive	....	21.	swam
9.	ate	22.	spent
10. have	....	23. take	....
11.	went	24. tell	....
12. lose	....	25.	wrote
13. make	....	26. get	....

17. Simple Past (Irregular Verbs)

150 Fill in the blanks with a verb from the box in the Simple Past.

break	swim	have	make	sit	write
buy	spend	drink	lose	wash	

1. She .. *made* .. a cake an hour ago.

2. She .... a hat last week.

3. The boy .... a letter yesterday.

4. They .... some plates a minute ago.

5. They .... in the sea for an hour.

6. They .... a lot of Coke last night.

7. She .... her arm last week.

8. He .... all his money last week.

9. She .... a bath two minutes ago.

10. He .... his wallet last night.

11. She .... on the old chair a minute ago.

12. She .... the clothes yesterday.

151 **Complete the sentences.**

Long form

1. I .. *did not* ... play tennis yesterday.
2. You .... go to the theatre.
3. He .... feed the dog.
4. They .... send a letter.
5. She .... find her keys.

Short form

I ... *didn't* ... play tennis yesterday.
You .... go to the theatre.
He .... feed the dog.
They .... send a letter.
She .... find her keys.

152 **Complete the sentences.**

	cut the grass	meet / friends	read a magazine	write a letter
Jane			✔	✔
Peter	✔	✔		
Pam & Ben	✔	✔		
Ann	✔			✔
You				

1. Jane .read a magazine and wrote a letter yesterday. She didn't cut the .
....grass or meet her friends yesterday. ....
2. Peter ....
....
3. Pam and Ben ....
....
4. Ann ....
....
5. I ....
....

17. Simple Past (Irregular Verbs)

153 **Look again at exercise 152, then ask and answer.**

1. Jane / meet / friends / yesterday? *Did Jane meet her friends yesterday? No, she didn't.*
2. Jane / cut the grass / yesterday? . . . .
3. Peter / write a letter / yesterday? . . . .
4. Peter / meet his friends / yesterday? . . . .
5. Pam and Ben / write a letter / yesterday? . . . .
6. Pam and Ben / meet their friends / yesterday? . . . .
7. Ann / write a letter / yesterday? . . . .
8. You / meet your friends / yesterday? . . . .
9. You / cut the grass / yesterday? . . . .
10. You / write a letter / yesterday? . . . .

154 **(a). Write what Jean did or didn't do yesterday.**

go shopping	
clean the house	✔
feed the cat	✔
telephone Mary	
watch a film on TV	
visit her grandparents	✔
take them a cake	✔

. . *Jean didn't go* . . . .
. . *shopping yesterday* . . . .

(b). Write what you did or didn't do yesterday.

155 **Fill in the blanks with the Simple Past of the verbs in brackets.**

Last Saturday my father . *took* . (take) my friends and me to the circus. We (1) . . . . (see)
lots of things. My father (2) . . . . (buy) us some popcorn and orange juice. We
(3) . . . . (eat) the popcorn and (4) . . . . (drink) the orange juice. We (5) . . . .
(laugh) at the funny clowns. There (6) . . . . (be) a lion-tamer. The lions (7) . . . . (do)
tricks; they (8) . . . . (jump) through hoops. A girl (9) . . . . (ride) an elephant
around the ring. We all (10) . . . . (have) a wonderful time.

156 **Choose the right verb, put it in the Simple Past and fill in the blanks.**

| write | drink | do | see | buy | sit | meet |
| drive | be | tell | come | take | cost | go |

Yesterday morning we 1) .. *went* .. to the market. We 2) .... our shopping baskets. Father 3) .... us there in the car. At the market, Mother 4) .... some fruit and vegetables. I 5) .... some birds that I wanted to buy. They 6) .... a lot of money. Mother 7) .... me they 8) .... too expensive. Then we 9) .... some friends and we all 10) .... to a café. We 11) .... at a table outside and 12) .... orange juice. Then Mother and I 13) .... home. In the afternoon I 14) .... my homework and 15) .... a letter to my grandmother.

157 **Complete the sentences with one word or phrase from the box.**

on Sundays	at the moment	in the evening	last week
usually	last night	tomorrow	
yesterday	every morning		two months ago

1. I .... *usually* .... walk to school.
2. We are going to visit them ....
3. Tom went to bed at 12 o'clock ....
4. She watches TV ....
5. You didn't come to school ....

6. We drink milk for breakfast ....
7. Father doesn't work ....
8. She wrote a letter to John ....
9. Don't go outside! It's raining ....
10. He telephoned me ....

158 **Put the verbs into the correct tense.**

1. She always ... *goes* .... (go) to church on Sunday.
2. I .... (buy) a new bicycle last week.
3. My family .... (go) to the theatre yesterday.
4. Tom .... (live) in London three years ago.
5. My mother .... (make) some coffee now.
6. Sam .... (go) to the circus tomorrow.
7. I .... (talk) on the telephone at the moment.
8. Sally always .... (help) her mother in the house.
9. I .... (have) dinner in a restaurant last Friday.

(159) Look at the pictures and complete the story.

Last night Mr West (1) .... a big dinner and (2) .... a lot of wine. He
(3) .... TV and then (4) .... to bed. At midnight he (5) .... a
noise at the door. He (6) .... the door and (7) .... a monster. The monster
(8) .... hungry. It (9) .... meat or fish. It (10) .... eating chairs,
tables and clothes. At first Mr West (11) .... what to do but then he (12) ....
the window and (13) .... out of it. He (14) .... his head and (15) ....
his leg. Suddenly he (16) .... up. He (17) .... on his bed. He
(18) .... on the floor. He (19) .... a headache but he (20) ....
happy. The monster (21) .... there. It (22) .... only a bad dream.

Now tell the class about a dream you had.

Game 20

The teacher divides the class into two groups. Then one student from group A starts a story
using Simple Past. Then a student from group B goes on with the story. The group that can't
go on with the story loses. Before starting the game the teacher should demonstrate how to
play it.

Group A S1 :   Last night Tony came back home late.
Group B S1 :   He had a bath and then ate dinner.
Group A S2 :   After that he watched TV.   etc.

18. Question Words (Who-Whose-What-When-Where-Why-How much/How many)

Some reporters are interviewing John Birch, a famous pop singer.

160 **Match the question words with the phrases as in the example :**

1. At the circus.	A. Who?	1. .... G ....
2. 8.30 pm.	B. When?	2. ....
3. A bird.	C. How much money?	3. ....
4. Twelve.	D. How many?	4. ....
5. Tony.	E. Why?	5. ....
6. Because she is clever.	F. Whose?	6. ....
7. On Monday.	G. Where?	7. ....
8. Ben's.	H. What time?	8. ....
9. £27.	I. What?	9. ....

18. Question Words

161 Fill in "Who", "Whose", "What", "When", "Where", "Why", "How much", "How many" or "What time".

1. .. *When?* ..... At 2:30.
2. .... ? At the cinema.
3. .... ? The teacher.
4. .... ? In the morning.
5. .... ? In the kitchen.
6. .... ? My brother's.
7. .... ? Because it's cold.
8. .... ? On Saturday.
9. .... ? In the classroom.
10. .... ? At the station.
11. .... ? John's.
12. .... ? An umbrella.

13. .... ? Sophia's.
14. .... ? Mary.
15. .... ? 10 o'clock.
16. .... ? Next Thursday.
17. .... ? Four.
18. .... ? In the park.
19. .... ? Mary's.
20. .... ? A car.
21. .... ? £45.
22. .... ? Tomorrow.
23. .... ? 8 pm.
24. .... ? A cup.

162 Choose the correct word.

1. .. *What* .. is it? It's a bird.
   A) Who   B) Where   C) What

2. .... is that radio? My father's.
   A) What   B) Whose   C) When

3. .... is that girl? My cousin.
   A) Who   B) Where   C) Whose

4. .... do you go to the shops?
   A) What   B) Whose   C) When

5. .... is the dog? In the garden.
   A) Whose   B) What   C) Where

6. .... are you late?
   A) What   B) Who   C) Why

7. .... is your sister's name?
   A) What   B) Who   C) Why

8. .... is it? It's 2 o'clock.
   A) Where   B) What time   C) When

9. .... does the film start?
   A) Who   B) When   C) What

10. .... speaks English?
   A) Who   B) Where   C) Why

163 Fill in the blanks with "Who", "Whose", "What", "When", "Where", "Why", "How much", "How many" or "What time".

1. .. *Why* ...... are you wearing a coat? Because it's cold.
2. .... is your party? On Saturday.
3. .... are these football boots? They're John's.
4. .... money have you got? £10.
5. .... is your school? It's near the station.

6. . . . . brothers have you got? Two brothers.
7. . . . . books have you got? Not many.
8. . . . . is he? He's Mr Smith.
9. . . . . are you reading that book? Because it's interesting.
10. . . . . people are there in this room? Twenty.
11. . . . . coat is this? It's John's.
12. . . . . does he come from? He comes from Brazil.
13. . . . . is your birthday? In January.
14. . . . . is it? 7.30.
15. . . . . are you running? Because I am late.
16. . . . . sugar is there? One kilo.
17. . . . . are you going tonight? To the cinema.
18. . . . . is he? In the kitchen.
19. . . . . girls are there? Twelve.
20. . . . . are they doing? They are watching TV.

(164) Fill in with "Who", "What", "Where", "When" or "What time".

1. . . . *Where* . . . . is the cheese? It's in the fridge.
2. . . . . is your party? On January 21st.
3. . . . . is your brother's name? Michael.
4. . . . . is that man? He's my uncle.
5. . . . . do you visit your grandparents? On Sundays.
6. . . . . have you got? A box of chocolates.
7. . . . . does this lesson finish? At eleven o'clock.
8. . . . . is the cat? It's on the chair.
9. . . . . can answer my question? I can.
10. . . . . is there in that bag? Some apples and oranges.

Game 21

Your teacher divides the class into two groups and then says words. The groups in turn say which question word matches the word said by the teacher. Each correct answer gets 1 point. The group with the most points is the winner.

Teacher :	at the station.	Group A S2 :	whose?
Group A S1 :	where?	Teacher :	Mary.
Teacher :	at noon.	Group B S2 :	whose?
Group B S1 :	when?	Teacher :	Wrong! Who! Group B doesn't get
Teacher :	Nick's.		a point.

19. Comparisons

You've got bigger ears than me.

Yes, but you've got a longer nose than me.

I am taller than you.

Yes, but I am stronger than you.

Wrong! I am stronger than you.

You are wrong! I am the strongest and the tallest of all of us.

| fat | fatter | the fattest |

Comparison of Adjectives

Adjectives	Positive	Comparative	Superlative
one syllable	long	longer than	the longest of / in
two syllables	happy	happier than	the happiest of / in
more than two syllables	beautiful	more beautiful than	the most beautiful of / in

Spelling — Adjectives ending in:

e + r / st	y ⟹ ier / iest	one stressed vowel between two consonants double the final consonant
large - larger - largest	heavy - heavier - heaviest	big - bigger - biggest BUT old - older - oldest

100

(165) Fill in the blanks.

1. short	*shorter* .. *the shortest.*	6. fat	
2. thin		7. small	
3. heavy		8. friendly	
4. funny		9. interesting	
5. old		10. careful	

Irregular Forms

Positive	Comparative	Superlative
good	better	best
bad	worse	worst
much	more	most
many / a lot	more	most
little	less	least

(166) Tommy, Tony and Terry are brothers. What do we know about them?

		Tommy	Tony	Terry
1.	polite	***	*	**
2.	lazy	*	***	**
3.	funny	**	*	***
4.	good	***	*	**
5.	friendly	*	**	***
6.	clever	***	*	**
7.	careful	**	***	*

1. Tony ..*is polite.*
   ...*Terry is more polite than Tony.*
   ...*Tommy is the most polite of all.*

2. Tommy

3. Tony

4. Tony

5. Tommy

6. Tony

7. Terry

19. Comparisons

167 Fill in the blanks with "than", "of" or "in".

1. My room is larger .. *than* ..... yours.
2. The white car is the fastest .... the three cars.
3. Watching TV is more interesting .... listening to the radio.
4. He is the best student .... his class.
5. She has got the most money .... all.
6. I've got more money .... you.
7. Summer is hotter .... winter.
8. Tom is the oldest .... all.
9. Winter is the coldest month .... the year.

168 Complete the sentences.

David	Tom	George

Age : 25	Age : 30	Age : 35
Weight : 70 kgs	Weight : 72 kgs	Weight : 75 kgs
Height : 1.68	Height : 1.72	Height : 1.80
Salary : £800/month	Salary : £1000/month	Salary : £1500/month
House : 3 rooms	House : 4 rooms	House : 5 rooms

1. (young) David is ... *younger than* ... Tom and George.
2. (old) George and Tom are .... David.
3. (heavy) George is the .... all.
4. (light) Tom is .... George.
5. (tall) Tom is .... David.
6. (tall) George is the .... all.
7. (old) George is .... Tom.
8. (little) David gets .... money .... Tom.
9. (much) George gets .... money .... Tom.
10. (small) David's house is .... Tom's.
11. (big) George's house is the .... all.
12. (big) Tom's house is .... David's.

169 **Complete the sentences as in the example :**

1. The red dress is
   ...the most..
   .expensive...
   of all. (expensive)

2. The clown with the
   red nose is ......
   ....
   than the other
   clown. (funny)

3. John is ....
   ....
   than Jim. (tall)

4. A horse is ......
   ....
   than a dog. (big)

5. Tina is ....
   ....
   than her brother.
   (short)

6. George is ......
   ....
   than James. (fat)

7. Sally is ....
   ....
   girl in the class.
   (beautiful)

8. A mouse is .....
   ....
   than a cat. (small)

9. Bert is ....
   ....
   of all. (tall)

10. The red T-shirt is
    ....
    ....
    of all. (expensive)

170 **Complete the sentences.**

1. (fast)   My car is .. *faster than*......... yours.
2. (thin)   She is the .... all.
3. (interesting) It is the .... book of the three of them.
4. (short)   Paula is .... Helen.

103

5. (difficult)   Mathematics is .... History.
6. (pretty)   She is the .... her class.
7. (happy)   Luca is .... Massimo.
8. (careful)   Tom is .... John.
9. (bad)   Don is the .... student .... class.
10. (beautiful)   Gloria is .... Angeles.

171 Compare yourself with Mary Taylor.

Name:	Mary Taylor		Name: ....

Age:	23		Age:	....
Height:	1.70 m		Height:	....
Weight:	55 kgs	Put your photo here	Weight:	....
House:	10 rooms		House:	....

1. Mary is *older than me.* ....
2. Mary is ....
3. Mary is ....
4. Mary's house is ....

Game 22a

1. Competition Game: Your teacher will divide the class into two groups and say an adjective. The groups, in turn, will tell him/her its comparative and superlative forms. Each correct answer gets 1 point. The group with the most points is the winner.

Teacher:	thin	Teacher:	big
Group A S1:	thinner - the thinnest	Group A S2:	more big - most big
Teacher:	boring	Teacher:	Wrong! bigger - the biggest
Group B S1:	more boring - the most boring		Group A doesn't get a point.

Game 22b

2. Your teacher will divide the class into two groups and say an adjective. The groups in turn say its opposite. Each correct answer gets 1 point. The group with the most points is the winner.

Teacher:	big	Teacher:	tall
Group A S1:	small	Group A S2:	small
Teacher:	young	Teacher:	Wrong! Short. Group A
Group B S1:	old		doesn't get a point.

Revision Exercises IV

172 Change to the plural as in the example :

1. That is an ox.   *Those are oxen..*   4. This is a goose. ....
2. I am a student. ....   5. He is a good doctor. ....
3. She is a woman. ....   6. That is a big box. ....

173 Fill in with "some" or "any".

1. There are ..*some*. glasses on the table.   4. There isn't .... Coke in the bottle.
2. Is there .... milk in the fridge?   5. Are there .... students in the
3. There is .... water in the glass.   classroom?

174 Fill in the blanks using "in", "at" or "on".

.. *On* .. Sunday.
1. .... the afternoon.
2. .... night.
3. .... 3 o'clock.

4. .... February 1st.
5. .... summer.
6. .... Easter.
7. ...... Thursday morning.

8. .... the morning.
9. .... 1992.
10. .... Christmas.
11. .... August.

175 Fill in the blanks with the Simple Present or Present Continuous.

Every day my father (1) .. *drives* .. (drive) to work. He (2) .... (work) in a bank. He (3) .... (like) his job. He (4) .... (get) up at seven o'clock every morning. He (5) .... (eat) his breakfast at the moment, and my mother (6) .... (make) some coffee. He always (7) .... (leave) home at half past seven. At the moment he (8) .... (laugh) because Ted, my brother, (9) .... (tell) him a joke.

176 Fill in "Who", "Whose", "What time", "Where" or "Why".

1. ..*What time* ..... is it? 8.30.
2. .... is this car? It's my father's.
3. .... is she? She's my sister.
4. .... is the milk? It's in the fridge.
5. .... are you wearing your coat? Because it is cold outside.
6. .... did she leave? At 6.20.

(177) **Look at the picture and complete the sentences with the correct preposition from the list below:**

next to	on	in front of	above
in	behind	between	under

Look at this pet shop. There is a goldfish bowl .... *on* ..... (1) the table. There is a goldfish .... (2) the bowl. The cat is .... (3) the bowl. The dog is .... (4) the table and .... (5) the goldfish bowl there is a bird in a cage. The goldfish bowl is .... (6) the cat and the box of dog biscuits. There's a ball .... (7) the plant. There's a mouse .... (8) the cat food.

(178) **Fill in "How much" or "How many".**

1. ... *How much* ....money have you got?
2. ....water is there in the bottle?
3. ....trees are there in the garden?
4. ....milk does the baby drink?
5. ....friends have you got?

179 **Some of the tenses of the underlined verbs are wrong.**
Find the mistakes and correct them.

John (1) waits for the bus now. He (2) takes the bus to school every morning because his school (3) was far away. It (4) is raining, so John (5) holds an umbrella. He (6) likes taking the bus because many of his friends (7) ride on it.

1. *..is waiting....*   2. ....   3. ....   4. ....
5. ....   6. ....   7. ....

180 **Fill in with Simple Past.**

Last Sunday we (1) . *went* . (go) on a picnic in the country. My mother (2) .... (drive) the car. My father (3) .... (sleep) all the way there because he (4) .... (be) tired. When we (5) .... (arrive) we (6) .... (run) straight to the river. We (7) .... (swim) for a long time and then we (8) .... (eat) our lunch. After lunch my father and I (9) .... (play) rugby. We (10) .... (leave) at six o'clock and (11) .... (go) home. We all (12) .... (have) a lovely time.

181 **Mary and Sam are talking about their last summer holidays.**
Fill in the blanks with the Simple Past.

Mary: Where (1) .. *did you go* ..... (you/go) on holiday last summer?
Sam: I (2) .... (go) to France to visit my cousins there.
Mary: How long (3) .... (you/stay)?
Sam: I (4) .... (stay) for two months and I (5) .... (have) a wonderful time. Where (6) .... (you/spend) your holidays?
Mary: We (7) .... (not/go) anywhere. My mother (8) .... (be) in hospital, so we (9) .... (stay) at home.
Sam: That's too bad!
Mary: Well, she (10) .... (come) home after three weeks, and we (11) .... (be) happy to see her.

182 **Put the verbs into the "Simple Present" or "Present Continuous".**

Donna: Hello, David. How .. *are* .. (be) you?
David: I (1) .... (be) fine, thanks!
Donna: (2) .... (be) your father at home?

David: No, he (3) .... (work) at the office. There (4) .... (be) no one at home. I (5) .... (be) alone.

Donna: Where (6) .... (be) everyone? What (7) .... (they / do)?

David: My mother (8) .... (shop) in town with my aunt. They (9) .... (buy) Christmas presents. My brother and sister (10) .... (play) in the park.

Donna: What (11) .... (you/do)?

David: I (12) .... (watch) television.

Donna: Please ask your mother or father to phone me later.

David: Okay. Bye.

Donna: Bye.

183 **Fill in the blanks and answer the questions as in the example:**

1. Look at .. *her!* ...
   . Is she. a singer? .
   No, she isn't. ....
   She is a teacher.

2. Look at ....!
   Are they geese?

   ....
   ....

3. Look at ....!
   Is he a doctor?

   ....
   ....

4. Look at ....!
   Is it a skirt?

   ....
   ....

184 **Fill in the blanks with "This", "These", "That" or "Those".**

1. .... are shoes.

2. .... is a chair.

3. .... is a bird.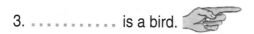

(185) **Find the differences in picture A using comparisons.**

<table>
<tr><td align="center">**Picture A**</td><td align="center">**Picture B**</td></tr>
</table>

1. *The dog is bigger. It has a longer tail and bigger ears.* ....

2. ....

....

3. ....

....

4. ....

....

5. ....

....

6. ....

....

7. ....

....

Revision Exercises IV

186 **Choose one verb from the box and fill in the blanks.**

have	hasn't got	lived	is	go	were	works	stays
had	live	didn't stay	are	was	didn't go	worked	

They 1) .. *live* .. in a big house in London. Mr Smith 2) .... in a school. He
3) .... a teacher. Mr and Mrs Smith 4) .... two children, Tina and Andrew. They
5) .... to school. They 6) .... very good students. Mrs Smith 7) .... at
home, she 8) .... a job now. Last year the family 9) .... in France. Mr Smith 10)
.... in an English school there, too. Their children 11) .... younger then so they
12) .... to school. They 13) .... a nanny to look after them because Mrs Smith
14) .... a job then. She 15) .... a secretary. She 16) .... at home. They
17) .... all a lot happier this year than they 18) .... in France last year.

187 **Choose the correct item.**

1. She .. A ..... now.
   A) is sleeping   B) sleeps   C) slept

2. They .... to the pub last night.
   A) are going   B) go   C) went

3. He .... some new clothes tomorrow.
   A) is going to buy   B) buys   C) bought

4. Look at her! She ....
   A) cries   B) is crying   C) cried

5. He .... up late yesterday.
   A) wakes   B) is waking   C) woke

6. We .... our grandparents tomorrow.
   A) visited   B) visit   C) are going to visit

7. Look! The cat .... up the tree.
   A) climb   B) is climbing   C) climbs

8. We .... to school yesterday.
   A) didn't go   B) don't go   C) aren't going

9. He .... a bath at the moment.
   A) has   B) had   C) is having

10. I .... a pair of shoes yesterday.
    A) buy   B) bought   C) am buying

188 **Find the mistakes and correct them.**

1. How many sugar do you want? .... *much* ....
2. There are some money on the table. ....
3. That car is my. ....
4. She is the better student in the class. ....
5. Who is it? It's a box. ....
6. That cars are red. ....
7. Carol and John is listening to the radio. ....
8. There are two waters on the table. ....
9. They not watch TV in the morning. ....
10. Jane don't like coffee. ....
11. Is these a dog? ....
12. She don't like spaghetti. ....
13. They is playing in the garden. ....
14. We has got a car. ....
15. That dress is her. ....

189 **Find the mistakes and correct them.**

1. Are there some cars in the street? ...*any*.........
2. The children is at home. ....
3. How much trees are there in the picture? ....
4. Tom having a bath. ....
5. She have got a watch. ....
6. Who is Sally? She is in the park. ....
7. They didn't came late last night. ....
8. She is oldest than her sister. ....
9. He don't like fish. ....
10. We never go to school in Sunday. ....
11. We didn't went to school yesterday. ....
12. How much books have you got? ....
13. She is the taller in her class. ....
14. There are any apples on the table. ....
15. When are the children? At school. ....

Irregular Verbs

Present	Explain the verbs in your mother tongue.	Past	Explain the verbs in your mother tongue.
am / is / are	....	was / were	....
break	....	broke	....
bring	....	brought	....
buy	....	bought	....
catch	....	caught	....
come	....	came	....
cost	....	cost	....
do	....	did	....
draw	....	drew	....
drink	....	drank	....
drive	....	drove	....
eat	....	ate	....
feed	....	fed	....
find	....	found	....
fly	....	flew	....
forget	....	forgot	....
get	....	got	....
give	....	gave	....
go	....	went	....
have	....	had	....
hit	....	hit	....
hurt	....	hurt	....
keep	....	kept	....
learn	....	learnt / -ed	....
leave	....	left	....
lose	....	lost	....
make	....	made	....
put	....	put	....
read	....	read	....
ride	....	rode	....
ring	....	rang	....
run	....	ran	....
see	....	saw	....
send	....	sent	....
sing	....	sang	....
sleep	....	slept	....
speak	....	spoke	....
spend	....	spent	....
swim	....	swam	....
take	....	took	....
teach	....	taught	....
tell	....	told	....
throw	....	threw	....
win	....	won	....